SOUTHERN LOCOMOTIVES TO SCALE

in this series by Ian Beattie

SOUTHERN LOCOMOTIVES TO SCALE

L.M.S.R. LOCOMOTIVES TO SCALE

B.R. STANDARD LOCOMOTIVES TO SCALE

G.W.R. LOCOMOTIVES TO SCALE

L.N.E.R. LOCOMOTIVES TO SCALE

SOUTHERN LOCOMOTIVES TO SCALE

IAN BEATTIE

D. BRADFORD BARTON LTD

MAJOR DIMENSIONS

CLASS	*NUMBER OF CYLINDERS*	*OVERALL LENGTH*	*OVERALL WIDTH*	*ENGINE WHEELBASE*	*BOILER PITCH*	*LEADING WHEELS (DIAMETER)*	*COUPLED WHEELS (DIAMETER)*	*TRAILING WHEELS (DIAMETER)*	*TENDER WHEELS (DIAMETER)*
KING ARTHUR 4-6-0	2	65′ 0$\frac{5}{8}$″	9′ 0″	27′ 6″	8′ 10$\frac{1}{2}$″	3′ 7″	6′ 7″	—	3′ 7″
N 2-6-0	2	57′ 6$\frac{3}{8}$″	8′ 10″	24′ 4″	8′ 3″	3′ 1″	5′ 6″	—	4′ 0″
L1 4-4-0	2	56′ 7$\frac{5}{8}$″	8′ 4″	24′ 3$\frac{1}{2}$″	8′ 7″	3′ 7″	6′ 8″	—	4′ 0″
LORD NELSON 4-6-0	4	69′ 9$\frac{3}{4}$″	8′ 9″	29′ 6″	9′ 2″	3′ 1″	6′ 7″	—	3′ 7″
U 2-6-0	2	57′ 9$\frac{5}{8}$″	8′ 10″	23′ 10″	8′ 6″	3′ 1″	6′ 0″	—	4′ 0″
U1 2-6-0	3	57′ 9$\frac{5}{8}$″	8′ 10″	23′ 10″	8′ 9″	3′ 1″	6′ 0″	—	4′ 0″
Z 0-8-0T	3	39′ 4″	8′ 10″	17′ 6″	8′ 6″	—	4′ 8″	—	—
V 4-4-0	3	58′ 9$\frac{3}{4}$″	8′ 6$\frac{1}{2}$″	25′ 6″	9′ 0″	3′ 1″	6′ 7″	—	3′ 10″
W 2-6-4T	2	44′ 0$\frac{1}{4}$″	8′ 6$\frac{1}{2}$″	36′ 4″	8′ 6″	3′ 1″	5′ 6″	3′ 1″	—
N 15 x 4-6-0	2	66′ 11$\frac{3}{4}$″	8′ 11″	27′ 4$\frac{1}{2}$″	8′ 11$\frac{1}{2}$″	3′ 6″	6′ 9″	—	3′ 7″
Q 0-6-0	2	53′ 9$\frac{1}{2}$″	8′ 4″	16′ 6″	8′ 6″	—	5′ 1″	—	4′ 0″
Q1 0-6-0	2	54′ 10$\frac{1}{2}$″	8′ 10″	16′ 6″	9′ 8″	—	5′ 1″	—	3′ 7″
WEST COUNTRY 4-6-2	3	67′ 4$\frac{3}{4}$″	8′ 5″	35′ 6″	9′ 7$\frac{3}{32}$″	3′ 1″	6′ 2″	3′ 1″	3′ 9″
U.S.A. 0-6-0T	2	29′ 6″	9′ 1$\frac{1}{2}$″	10′ 0″	7′ 6″	—	4′ 6″	—	—
MERCHANT NAVY 4-6-2	3	71′ 7$\frac{3}{4}$″	8′ 10$\frac{3}{4}$″	36′ 9″	9′ 5$\frac{7}{32}$″	3′ 1″	6′ 2″	3′ 7″	3′ 7″

6187/3BL ISBN 0 85153 389 2
printed in Great Britain by Lovell Baines Print Ltd., Newbury, Berkshire and bound by Robert Hartnoll Ltd., Bodmin, for the publishers
D. BRADFORD BARTON LTD TRETHELLAN HOUSE TRURO CORNWALL ENGLAND

CONTENTS

drawings to 4mm to 1 foot scale, except for those showing details

LIVERY AND INSIGNIA

Two shades of green were utilised during the existence of the S.R.; 'S.R. Green' during Maunsell's incumbency and a lighter, 'Malachite Green' by Bulleid, the latter applied to appropriate classes as they passed through the works on repair or heavy overhaul. In general, the paint scheme for passenger locomotives was as follows:

Green: Boiler, cab, tender sides and rear, running plate valances, wheel splashers, locomotive wheel spokes and hubs (including Bulleid-Firth-Brown variety), step backing plates, cylinders in some instances. Black: All structural parts not finished in green; smokebox, cab roof, running plate surfaces. Red: Buffer beams and stocks. Polished metal: Motion linkage and rodding, brass external pipework. Lining: Passenger locomotives with boiler bands lined black sandwiched by white, single white lining outlining cab, tender sides and rear panels, running plate valances, splashers, step backing plates; cylinders in some instances.

NAMEPLATES: Buffed brass letters in 'gill sans serif' script, brass surround, red background. Size of letters vary, size and shape of plate according to fitment. Class title in small appendage beneath main plate except on locomotives bearing name from which class took title.

NUMBERS:
Maunsell era: unshaded yellow, bold serif type, either side of tender below company name and on righthand side of front buffer beam.
Bulleid era: on repainting to malachite green, gill sans serif numbers, unshaded, on cab sides and righthand side of front buffer beam.
Bulleid locomotives: gill sans type, on cab sides and central above buffer beam (4-6-2s), righthand side of front buffer beam (Q.1).

NUMBERING SYSTEM, BULLEID CLASSES: For his own locomotive designs, Bulleid introduced the Continental style of numbering, for example:
Pacifics, 21C24 (2 = two leading axles, 1 = one trailing axle, C = three coupled axles, 24 = engine number)
Q.1 Class, C15 (C = three coupled axles, 15 = engine number)
These numbers were rendered in gold, shaded red to right.

INSIGNIA: Throughout the existence of the S.R., the single word 'Southern' was employed without crest or other innovations:
Tender locomotives: either side of the tender; in Maunsell days the title was set relatively high on the sheets, beneath which was the engine number; Bulleid moved the number to cab sides and the company name was positioned more centrally on the tender.
Tank locomotives: high on tank sides, above number.

LETTERS:
Maunsell era: matching the number style, i.e., unshaded yellow in bold serif script.
Bulleid era: gill sans serif, unshaded yellow. In several cases both letters and numbers were outlined in olive green.
Bulleid locomotives: as per numbers, i.e., gold, shaded red to right, gill sans serif type.

LIVERIES:
'King Arthur' Class 4-6-0, 1924; Green livery, including cylinders, fully lined.
N Class 2-6-0, 1924: Green livery, S.E.C.R., dull grey all over.
L.1 Class 4-4-0, 1926: Green, fully lined.
'Lord Nelson' Class 4-6-0, 1926: Green livery, including cylinders in Maunsell era, fully lined.
U Class 2-6-0, 1928: Green, fully lined.
U.1 Class 2-6-0, 1928: Green, fully lined.
Z Class 0-8-0T, 1929: Black overall, single green lining surrounding tank, cab and bunker sides.
'Schools' Class 4-4-0, 1930: Green, fully lined.
W Class 2-6-4T, 1931: Black overall, single green line surrounding tank, cab and bunker sides, also running plate valances, cylinders and upper front buffer beam (painted black).
'Remembrance' Class 4-6-0, 1934: Green livery including cylinders, fully lined.
Q Class 0-6-0, 1938: Black overall.
Q.1 Class 0-6-0, 1942: Black overall.
'West Country' 4-6-2, 1945: Malachite green casing with triple horizontal yellow bands. Nameplates mostly accompanied by brass plaques of crests, etc., plus additional plates proclaiming class. Cab roof and top surface of boiler casing black.
U.S.A. Class 0-6-0T, 1946: Black overall, unlined.
Rebuilt 'Merchant Navy' Class 4-6-2, 1941-1956: Full B.R. express passenger livery: green boiler, cab, tender, running plate valances, cylinders, lined in black sandwiched by orange lines. Black elsewhere. Background colour of nameplates red, but many repainted black by B.R. Number plate on smokebox door, number decals on cab sides; B.R. logo on tender sides.

ADDITIONAL NOTES
S.R. smoke deflectors rendered in black; isolated examples were experimentally panelled in green.
All S.R. engines were painted black during World War II; the early 'Merchant Navy' 4-6-2s were turned out in matt malachite green initially, but were repainted black until 1945.

This volume is one of a series of five reviewing steam motive power designs emanating from the four Groups and British Railways. It sets out to identify and portray the various locomotive classes built – though not necessarily conceived – during the quarter-century existence of the Southern Railway, from establishment in 1923 to dissolution in 1948.

By means of scale line drawings, complementary photographs, biographical summaries and major dimensions, the information presented herein is directed towards rail enthusiasts of all ages and degrees of knowledge, with perhaps a bias towards those who are in the throes of building or already possess model railways, for whom the dimensional and allied details given should save much time and effort in researching their favourite S.R. engine. No pretension towards microscopic examination of every aspect of each locomotive is claimed, rather the broader view is the criterion; the experienced modeller wishing to construct a replica locomotive depicting a particular period of usage is advised to consult specialised publications for precise specifications of auxiliary fitments, livery, insignia and numbering systems customary at the chosen point in time.

Much the smallest of the four Groups instituted at the beginning of 1923 by provision of the Railways Act of 1921, the Southern Railway was primarily a passenger-carrying concern with a relatively low-key freight operation, being the only one whose revenue was principally derived from passenger transportation. This concentration arose from three crucial aspects inherited by the company – the presence of many holiday resorts on the long southern coastline served by the railway, from Kent to Devon and North Cornwall, to which millions flocked each summer; an extremely busy suburban commuter system into London, in which steam was progressively supplanted by electric traction so that eventually the S.R. possessed the largest electrified suburban network in the world; and the traffic flowing to and from Channel ports at Folkestone, Dover and Newhaven, together with the wholly-owned international port at Southampton.

Composed mainly of three previously autonomous companies, the London & South Western, London Brighton & South Coast and South Eastern & Chatham Railways, the S.R. was administered in three divisions corresponding to the territories of the former systems – the Western, Central and Eastern Sections respectively. The enterprising L.S.W.R.'s sphere of influence had extended from London (Waterloo) into Hampshire – the company had built the huge Southampton Docks complex – and westwards throughout Dorset and Devon to Padstow on the North Cornish coast. The expansionist activities of the line in the South West during the nineteenth century had aroused the animosity of the G.W.R. and for decades the rival companies tried to outvie each other in promoting ever faster express services between London and the then-thriving steamship port of Plymouth; where the two lines intertwined – at Exeter for instance – the L.S.W.R. was compelled to rely on the benevolence of the older-established company in the matter of running rights, an arrangement which all too often led to frustrating delays and acrimony.

Serving a far more compact area than its rambling westerly neighbour, the L.B.S.C.R. operated within an approximate triangle bounded by London, Portsmouth and Hastings; a massive commuter operation was the major source of income which in conjunction with the renumerative services to the popular seaside towns situated within L.B.S.C.R. territory provided a financial stability that belied the company's size. The L.B.S.C.R. held the distinction of being the sole railway in Britain to site locomotive erecting shops in a coastal resort, at Brighton.

Strictly speaking, the S.E.C.R. was not a railway company at all. The S.E.C. Railways' Managing Committee, from which the S.E.C.R. title arose, had administered the independent South Eastern and London Chatham & Dover Railways since 1899, following a half-century of bitter feuding, uneconomic installation of lines and continually degenerating standards of operation; by the mid-1890s the management and maintenance of both railways were so chaotic that a merger of interests was forced through sheer necessity. So successful was the scheme that in the Edwardian era the combined result had been transformed into a model of efficiency and presentation. Encompassing the county of Kent, parts of Surrey and Sussex, the S.E.C.R. brought to the Southern the lucrative traffic generated by the Kentish cross-Channel ports in addition to a comprehensive suburban network.

In common with the L.M.S. and L.N.E.R., the S.R. was initially subjected to internal dissension via the loyalties and practical methods of staff hailing from the three former companies; however, under the highly effective leadership of Sir Herbert Walker, appointed General Manager in 1924 from a similar position on the L.S.W.R., the new company took on its own identity in which all hands worked towards the same goal, that of moulding a disparate and somewhat under-financed organisation into a unified, efficient and presentable entity.

Overall electrification of suburban services commenced soon after the act of Grouping, and the consequent disruption to commuter traffic created a great deal of adverse publicity in the early days. In counteraction, Walker formed a vigorous public relations department, the first of its kind within a major railway, headed by newspaperman John Elliot, a magnetic personality who motivated and sustained a series of brilliantly successful countrywide publicity programmes that kept the S.R., whatever its shortcomings, in the public eye.

Of the three Chief Mechanical Engineers superintending the main line systems incorporated into the Group and therefore eligible for appointment to lead the engineering fortunes of the combine, two (Lawson Billinton, L.B.S.C.R.; and Robert Urie, L.S.W.R.) were approaching retirement in 1923, so that the well-regarded C.M.E. of the S.E.C.R. was selected to the post of S.R. locomotive leadership. Aged 54 at the time, Richard E.L. Maunsell was a Dubliner of volatile temperament with a distinguished record of constructional and organisational achievements. Trained on the Great Southern & Western Railway of Ireland on which he eventually rose to become locomotive superintendent, Maunsell took over engineering supremacy of the S.E.C.R. in 1913, based at the Ashford headquarters of that concern. Whilst controlled by a centralised committee, the two railway companies (S.E.R. and L.C.D.R.) maintained their independence up to Grouping insofar as the directors and shareholders were concerned; however, the responsibility for provision of motive power and rolling stock on both systems fell on Maunsell's capable shoulders, as it had done on his predecessors' since 1899.

Into the S.R. with Maunsell came a strong team of S.E.C. development specialists, many of whom had originated with the G.W.R., including H. Holcroft. Maunsell's tenure of office was persistently constrained by inadequate funds and the vagaries of permanent way installation and maintenance over the network. The latter brought him into conflict with a strict Civil Engineer who could not sanction several advanced locomotive designs stemming from Maunsell's fertile brain in the quest for improved performance, and the general paucity of capital prevented the replacement of a host of uneconomic inherited classes. In more equable conditions, Maunsell may well have been placed alongside Gresley, Churchward and Stanier in the front ranks of steam locomotive engineers. Because of ill-health and advancing age, Maunsell retired in the autumn of 1937, in his seventieth year.

Oliver V.S. Bulleid was appointed C.M.E. in succession to Maunsell, following a near-lifetime on the G.N.R. and subsequent L.N.E.R.; born in New Zealand of a Devonian family, he had for fourteen years acted as chief assistant to Sir Nigel Gresley. That Bulleid was a complete individual in both personality and technological instincts is borne out by the record of highly radical designs he pursued for the S.R. Coincidentally the same age on appointment as Maunsell had been in 1923, Bulleid introduced just four locomotive classes in his eleven-year premiership, yet the impact created was out of all proportion to their numbers. Revelling in the controversy, speculation—and almost disbelief—surrounding his Pacific, Q.1 and 'Leader' designs, Bulleid thereby contrived to bring much-needed new publicity to the S.R., which, suffering by comparison with the other three Groups in the dearth of top link express engines and ultra-fast services, had acquired a somewhat pedantic reputation in the late 1930s. The unique double-ended 'Leader' Class 0-6-6-0 proved too revolutionary in the atmosphere prevailing at its debut in 1949, and after fruitless but costly experimentation the two prototypes were scrapped. By this time Bulleid had left for pastures new, his individuality being at odds with the aims of the British Railways Executive formed on Nationalisation in 1948; his remaining years of activity centred around an ingenious turf-burning design for the Irish state network, Coras Iompair Eireann.

URIE/MAUNSELL 'KING ARTHUR' CLASS 4-6-0, 1924

At the outset of his career with the S.R., Maunsell was presented with a substantial challenge; to supply a fleet of express passenger locomotives for main line duties, chiefly on the Western Section where there was a critical shortage of top link power. So acute was the demand that there was no time to prepare and prove a wholly new proposal, therefore the C.M.E. adeptly chose as a basis R.W. Urie's worthy 1918-vintage two-cylinder 4-6-0 blueprint, to which twenty locomotives had been erected by the L.S.W.R. prior to Grouping.

Maunsell considerably improved the front-end characteristics by applying Churchward's epochal valve travel and steam passage principles – Maunsell had been the first engineer outside the G.W.R. to employ these techniques, on designs fulfilled whilst in harness with the S.E.C.R. – and ordered ten new locomotives from the ex-L.S.W.R. erecting shops at Eastleigh, near Southampton. Fortuitously, an authorisation for rebuilding a number of elderly L.S.W.R. 4-6-0s, stemming from the days of Dugald Drummond – a dour Scot who had governed the L.S.W.R. motive power scene with a rule of iron from 1895 till his death in 1912 – was outstanding from the immediate pre-Grouping period, so that Maunsell was able to redirect the programme in favour of his revised Urie design. The locomotives were duly outshopped in 1924-25, bearing many typical L.S.W.R. features, including cabs and auxiliary boiler fitments (namely centre-locked smokebox doors, and boiler-side handrails continued over the smokebox front faces); the numbering series, bogies and celebrated Drummond inside-framed bogie tenders (affectionately termed 'water-carts') were drawn from the Drummond 4-6-0s, which were scrapped simultaneously with the Eastleigh construction schedule. At much the same time, the twenty original Urie 4-6-0s were converted to Maunsell's specification.

A further thirty examples came from the North British Locomotive Company of Glasgow in 1925, and to complete the class fourteen more emerged from Eastleigh in 1926-27; these 44 engines differed from the initial versions in having S.E.C.R.-style cabs (of Midland inspiration), smokebox doors sealed by peripheral tabs and boiler handrails severed short of the smokebox faces. Tenders utilised were the L.S.W.R.-type, large-capacity outside-framed bogie variety – unlike the other three Groups, the S.R. lacked water trough facilities, thus large tenders were de rigueur on long-distance services – and for the final batch of Eastleigh-built engines, which were distributed onto the Central Section where relatively small-diameter turntables abounded, a six-wheel pattern was provided. Officially designated 'N.15', the members of the 74-strong class were individually given names connected with the legend of King Arthur and the Knights of the Round Table, adroitly seized upon by the S.R. publicity machine in bringing the class to public awareness.

Beyond the fitting of effective smoke deflectors, an innovation applied to each S.R. tender locomotive (bar 0-6-0s) from 1933 onwards, and adjustments to the smokebox fittings of the earlier builds in conformity with the majority of the class, the 'King Arthur' 4-6-0s remained substantially as outshopped until B.R. times. The smokebox-mounted dual super-heater relief valves (frequently referred to as 'snifters') characteristic of all Maunsell engines were then deleted, and 'water-cart' tenders were replaced by more youthful substitutes.

Despite their original role as interim hauliers prior to introduction of the 'Lord Nelson' Class, the 'King Arthurs' good performance and formidable reliability even under the worst conditions guaranteed enduring utility, although electrification of many Central Section passenger services in the mid-1930s caused dissemination of many 'King Arthurs' away from the area of some of their finest working.

The denouement arrived in the early 1950s: the wide route availability of the newly-completed, extremely energetic Bulleid lightweight Pacific Class caused wholesale withdrawal of the older Maunsell two-cylinder 4-6-0s, of which the first to go, between 1953 and 1957, were the original L.S.W.R.-built versions. The B.R. policy of dieselisation put paid to the rest of the class by 1963, with a single representative – No.777 'Sir Lamiel' (built in Glasgow in 1925) being selected for preservation.

One of the initial Eastleigh 'King Arthurs' complete with L.S.W.R. cab and soon-to-be-replaced Drummond 'water-cart' tender, No.30455 'Sir Lancelot' poses at Nine Elms sheds, serving Waterloo, in April 1955. (F. Hornby)

Tender from Drummond G14 class.

URIE/MAUNSELL 'KING ARTHUR' CLASS 4-6-0, 1924

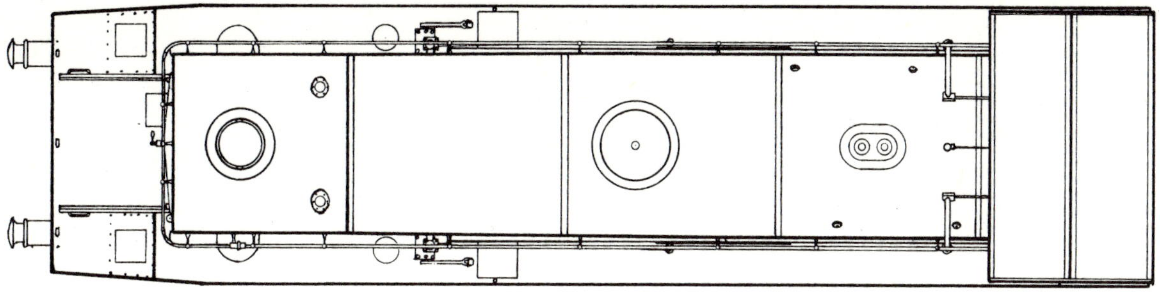

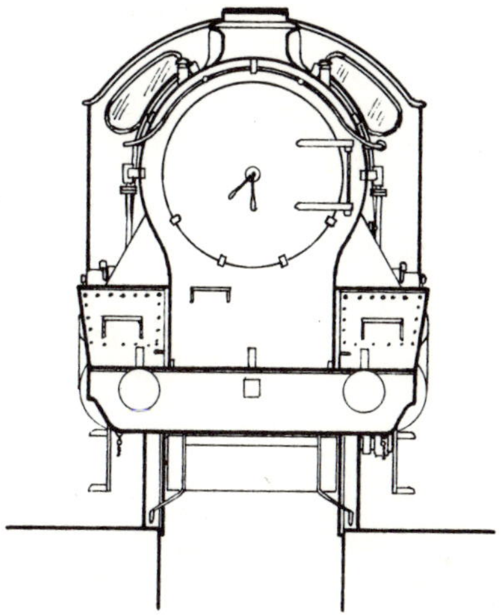

URIE/MAUNSELL 'KING ARTHUR' CLASS 4-6-0, 1924

11

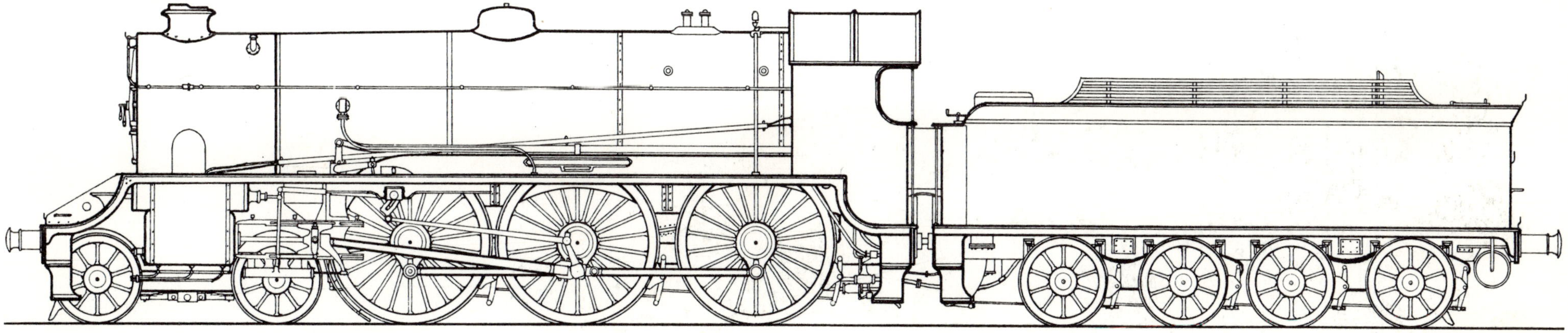

Numbers 448 to 457

Drumond tender

FOUR MAUNSELL SMOKE DEFLECTION EXPERIMENTS
(Conducted mid-to-late 1920s: 'King Arthur' Class)

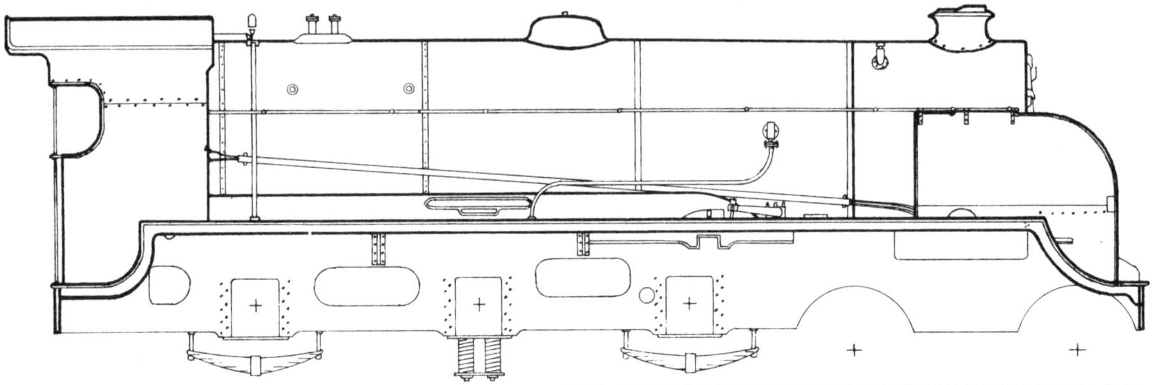

VERSION OF 1925 ONWARDS, INCLUDING MAUNSELL CAB AND SMOKEBOX FITTINGS. DEFLECTORS FROM MID-1930s. FRAME DETAILS BASICALLY COMMON TO ENTIRE CLASS

Numbers 763 to 806

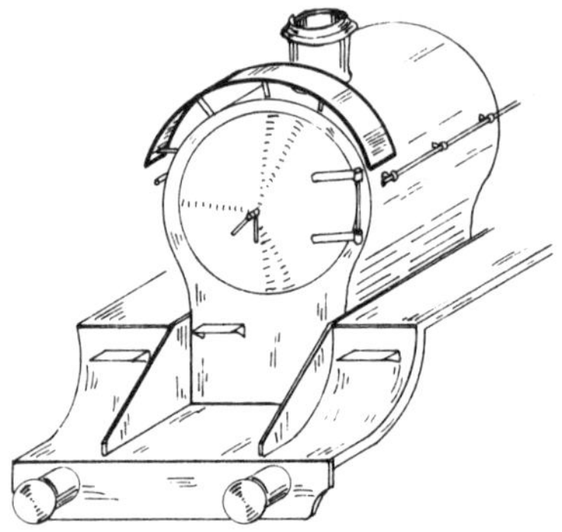

No.753 Melisande
Curved attachment cresting smokebox front face

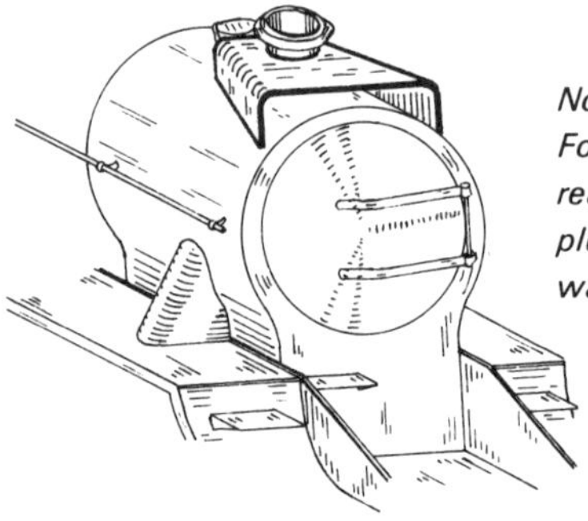

No.783 Sir Gillemere
Following experiment with a shovel-shaped fitting to rear of chimney on No.450 Sir Kay, a similar fitting plus a casing, with open ends, surrounding chimney was tried on No.783

12

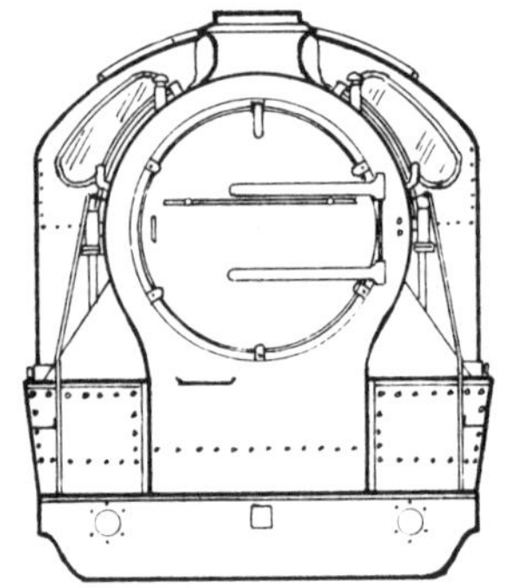

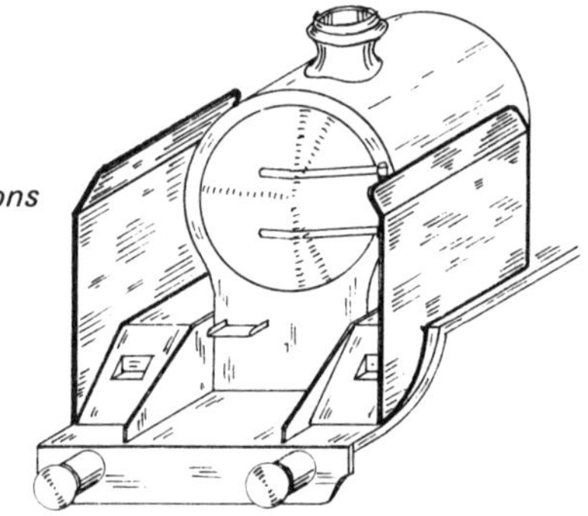

No.772 Sir Percivale
Continental-style 'Elephant Ear' deflectors; successful, but unnecessarily large for Southern operating conditions

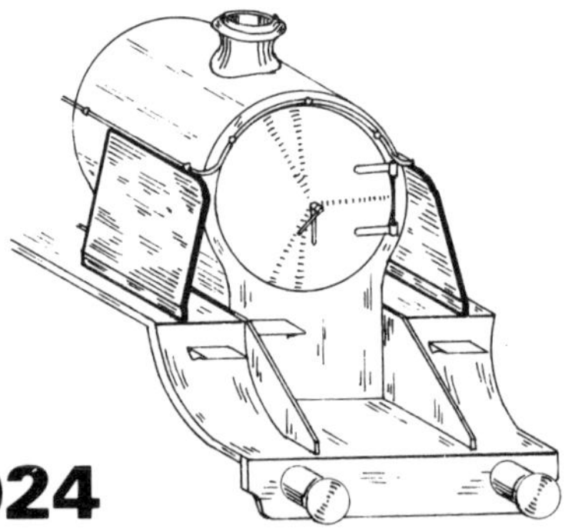

No.453 King Arthur
Small smokebox-side deflectors. Final experiment in series; Maunsell designed standardised deflectors midway in size between these and the 'Elephant Ear' variety

URIE/MAUNSELL
'KING ARTHUR' CLASS 4-6-0, 1924

MAUNSELL N CLASS 2-6-0, 1924

Altogether a most successful and versatile mixed traffic class, Maunsell's N 2-6-0 traced its origins back prior to the outbreak of World War I on the S.E.C.R., designed in response to a requirement for an engine sufficiently powerful to mitigate the wasteful practice of double-heading then common with comparatively small 0-6-0s. Whilst the war prevented construction of a prototype until 1917, the outcome was nonetheless a thoroughly advanced locomotive for the period, owing much of its composition to G.W.R. influences, reflected externally by a Belpaire firebox, domeless tapered boiler and top-feed mechanism – the 'dome' contained the latter – together with a cab and tender of evident Midland Railway derivation. The dearth of S.E.C.R. financial resources at that time resulted in a limited construction programme, commencing three years after appearance of the prototype and ceasing at Grouping with fifteen examples in service.

The versatility and low running costs of the N Class Moguls were recognised by the Government of the day, in a plan calculated to alleviate the prospect of unemployment in a huge munitions complex following the end of World War I, and to prepare for possible Nationalisation of the railways: complete sets of parts for assembling a hundred 2-6-0s were commissioned from Woolwich Arsenal. Before completion of the order, however, the Railways Act in the meantime having provided for Grouping in lieu of the expected Nationalisation, the newly-created Groups proved reluctant to purchase these Government inspired 'kits' and work thereon ground to a halt.

Eventually a number of locomotives were assembled from the mass of parts by the Metropolitan Railway and also by Maunsell's native company, the G.S. & W.R. of Ireland; fifty sets were acquired at knockdown prices by the S.R. and erected at Ashford in 1924-25. The utility of these and the S.E.C.R. N Class engines prompted a further, purely S.R.-built batch of fifteen replicas emerging in 1932-34, equipped with 4,000-gallon, six-wheel tenders in place of the 3,500-gallon variety attached to the earlier Moguls. Except for the final eight of the last batch, which were built for lefthand driving, the Moguls conformed to the former S.E.C.R. custom of righthand drive.

Available throughout the S.R. network over a wide range of duties, from semi-fast passenger to stopping goods, the N Class 2-6-0s were trouble-free and easy-steaming hauliers capable, by virtue of excellent tractive effort obtained through a combination of high-capacity boilers and small coupled wheels, of handling exceptionally heavy loads – an asset vital during World War II when circumstances demanded movement of enormous train rakes.

Subjected to much experimentation in the late 1920s and 1930s on generally abortive projects such as feed-water heating, novel valve motions and water condensing equipment, the eighty Moguls were otherwise little altered under S.R. ownership, beyond the obligatory installation of smoke deflectors. Many of the earlier examples sported tail rods – rare features on British locomotives, being extensions of piston rods projecting forward of the cylinder front covers to render enhanced support for the pistons, but fraught with sealing difficulties. These were removed in the 1930s; the lack of front steps on the S.E.C.R.-built engines was also rectified. A three-cylinder development provided additional power for minimal increase in coal and water consumption; classified N.1, these locomotives were in direct competition with the firmly established U.1 Class and consequently only six were built.

Under B.R. auspices, several 2-6-0s were equipped with updated cylinder and front-end arrangements; however, the imminent withdrawal of steam traction forced abandonment of the scheme. Arguably the hardest-worked and most durable constituents of the S.R. motive power roster, the N Moguls were progressively condemned to oblivion from 1962 onwards, the last survivor disappearing in 1966.

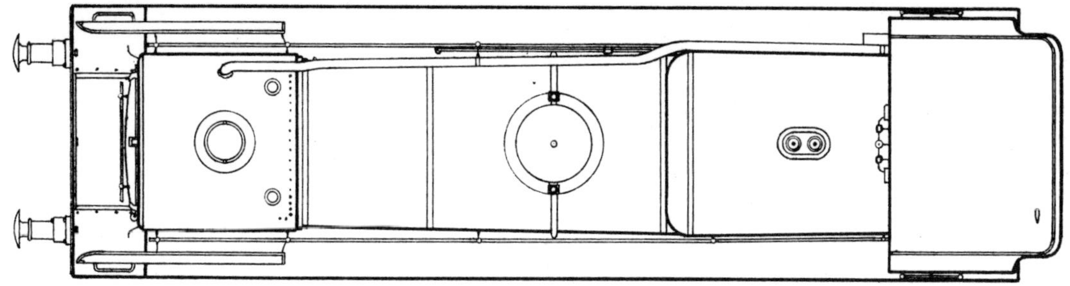

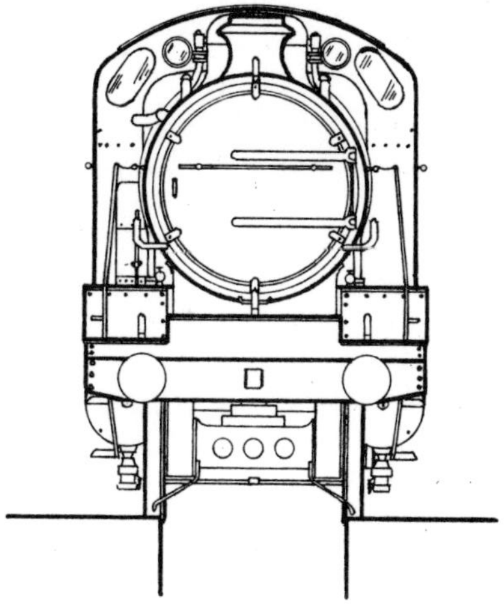

MAUNSELL N CLASS 2-6-0, 1924

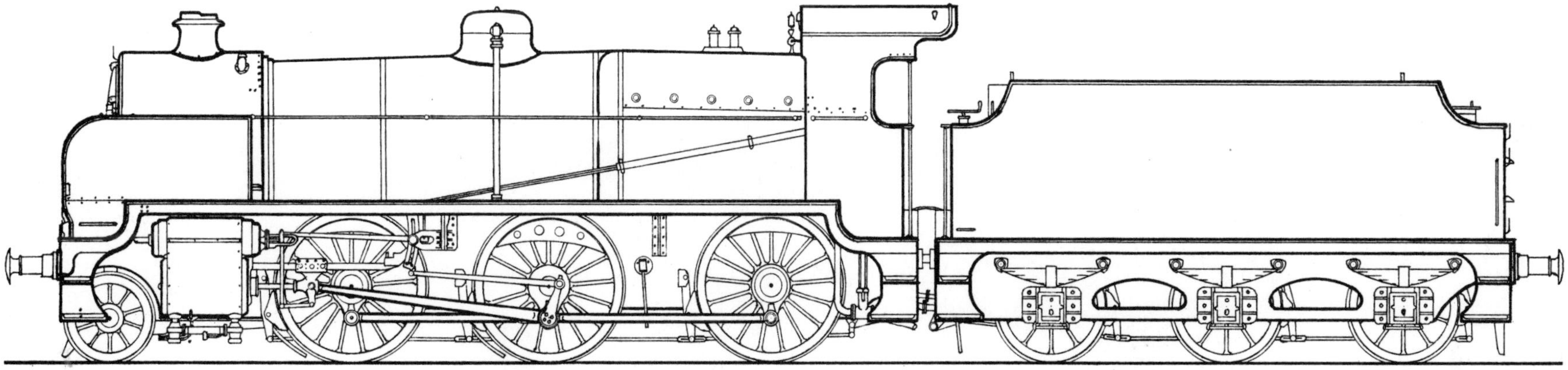

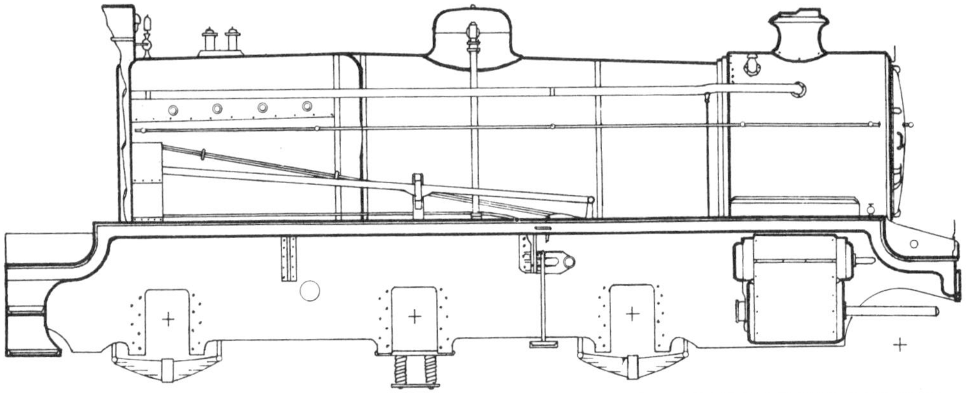

AS ORIGINALLY BUILT, WITHOUT DEFLECTORS OR FRONT STEPS. NOTE PISTON TAIL ROD AND STEP ATTACHED TO EXPANSION LINK BRACKET

A fine study of 1924-vintage No.31844 pausing at Barnstaple with a van train in June 1960. Note the position of reverse rod and brake ejector exhaust pipe, indicating righthand drive. (N.L. Browne)

MAUNSELL N CLASS 2-6-0, 1924

Steadily growing passenger traffic over the Eastern Section of the S.R. in the early 1920s necessitated ever weightier trains which gradually undermined the capabilities of the ex-S.E.C.R. 4-4-0 classes assigned thereto, the most youthful of which were a series outshopped in 1914. Several members of this, the L Class, had ironically been delivered by Borsig of Berlin just in time to augment the war effort against Germany. The failure of these locomotives to cope adequately with the growth of services provoked an urgent re-appraisal of motive power, resulting in an order for machines of much enhanced power consistent with a relatively light weight in view of restricted axle load limits over various sections of ex-S.E.C.R. permanent way.

In a sequence of events identical to the genesis of the 'King Arthur' Class, Maunsell was unable to develop a design from scratch in the time available and therefore opted to modify the L Class specifications, which had originated with H.S. Wainwright, his predecessor on the S.E.C.R. The North British Locomotive Company accepted the contract to manufacture fifteen locomotives in short order and all were duly delivered in 1926. Logically classified L.1, the Maunsell 4-4-0s exhibited a similar tractive effort to their progenitors; however, the use of higher boiler pressures, improved superheating and superior valve design ensured greater power and efficiency in operation, facets that were truly proven on the Channel boat trains for which the class was destined.

Externally the L.1s bore a remarkable resemblance to the classical M.R. simple and compound 4-4-0s and subsequent L.M.S. 2P 4-4-0s,locomotives that to many enthusiasts are the culmination of the traditionally elegant outline of British 4-4-0s. Driven from the righthand side of the cab in accordance with former S.E.C.R. practice, the L.1s were popular with their crews for their considerable turn of speed, excellent free-steaming qualities and general easiness of driving. Akin to all S.R.-owned 4-4-0 locomotives, barring the later 'Schools' Class, the L.1s were not equipped with smoke deflectors.

Prior to Grouping, Maunsell had successfully updated Wainwright's earlier 4-4-0 designs, the D and E Classes, and these bolstered the L and L.1 engines in maintaining the principal express duties on the Eastern Section until strengthening work on main line structures permitted heavier, more potent locomotives to share the burden.

Electrification of their native routes in the 1950s caused the transference of several L.1s onto the Western Section, the remainder being put into indefinite 'mothballs' from which they never re-emerged. Withdrawals began in earnest in 1959, and by the end of 1961 all fifteen 4-4-0s had vanished into the locomotive graveyards.

The neat, uncluttered lines of the archetypally English L.1 Class 4-4-0s finely displayed by No.31755, captured at Ashford in May 1958. (F. Hornby)

MAUNSELL L1 CLASS 4-4-0, 1926

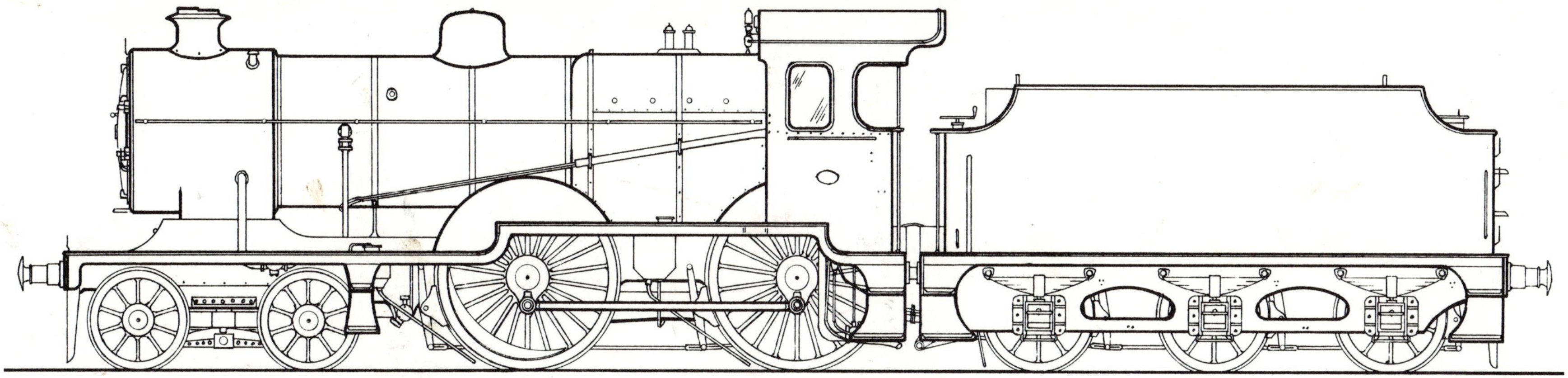

MAUNSELL L1 CLASS 4-4-0, 1926

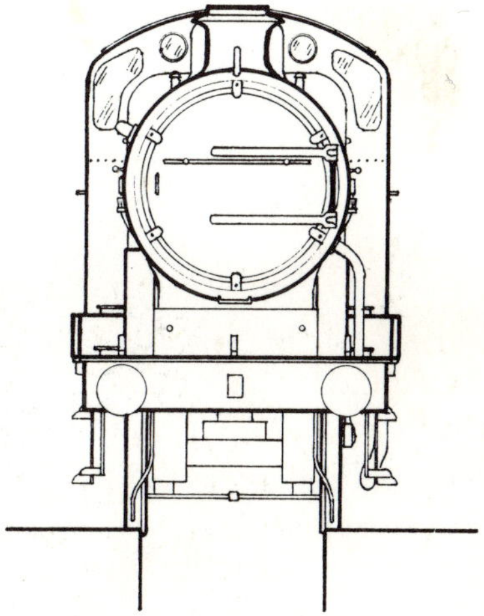

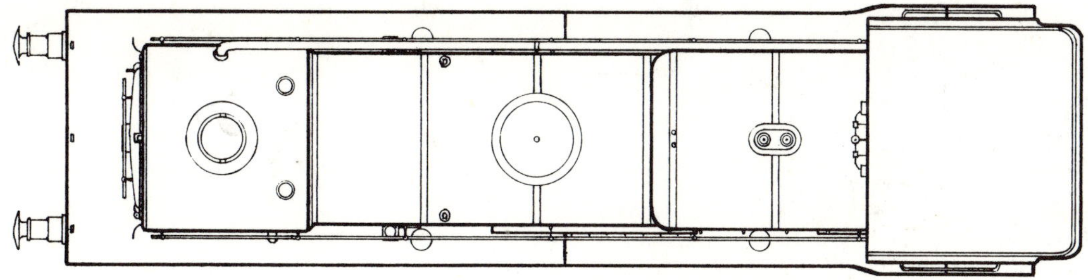

MAUNSELL 'LORD NELSON' CLASS 4-6-0, 1926

The largest and most powerful S.R. express locomotives before the appearance of Bulleid's revolutionary Pacifics in the 1940s, the superbly proportioned 'Lord Nelson' Class 4-6-0s exhibited in full measure the smoothness, reliability and ease of control characteristic of Maunsell's designs. Yet they contrived to lack the overall breadth of performance expected from such a carefully considered specification, into which the C.M.E. and his assistants had poured every ounce of technological skill and ingenuity. The prototype took to the rails in 1926 and underwent protracted trials, following which assembly began in earnest in 1928. Because of the operational shortcomings, the building programme was terminated in 1929 after a total of only sixteen 'Lord Nelsons', all named after famous naval personalities, had been outshopped. All things being equal, the traffic department would have welcomed a much larger fleet, and Maunsell subsequently embarked on an ambitious but ultimately abortive 4-6-2 proposal.

Some ten years after the class was completed, Bulleid introduced a series of major adaptations including replacement cylinders, and reworked blasting arrangements in the form of Lemaitre multiple-blast pipes, externally distinguished by immensely broad chimneys, which provided that much-sought extra sparkle to the performance and thereby justified the locomotives' existence via some truly spirited feats of haulage. On many occasions 'Lord Nelsons' took over premier express trains from failed Bulleid Pacifics, until the vastly uprated dependability of the rebuilt versions sapped the utility of the big 4-6-0s in this sphere.

Harking back to the Maunsell era, the 'Lord Nelson' design broke new ground in possessing four cylinders so arranged to give eight power strokes per driving wheel revolution as opposed to the conventional four strokes – an invention of the ubiquitous Harry Holcroft – the primary factor in the exceptionally smooth and untemperamental power delivery of the engines. The remarkably high calculated tractive effort figure was seized upon by the vigilant S.R. publicity machine in 1926 to hail the new product as the most potent locomotive in Britain. This claim stung the G.W.R., foremost exponents of the highly-advanced top link 4-6-0, into launching the ultimate 'King' Class a year later.

Maunsell magnanimously supplied details of his 'Lord Nelson' specification to the L.M.S. – an act which inadvertently provoked a fortunately shortlived spate of acrimony between senior officers of the two systems – in response to Fowler's desperate search for a modern express design, materialising in the renowned 'Royal Scot' Class based largely on Maunsell's brainchild.

Whilst primarily intended for working heavy boat trains between London and Dover, the various secondary duties delegated to the 4-6-0s and their acknowledged deficiency in performance prompted numerous experimental alterations. Amongst these, No.860 'Lord Hawke' was equipped with a boiler slightly longer than standard, the crank mechanism of No.865 'Sir John Hawkins' was modified to deliver the orthodox four power strokes per wheel revolution, and No.859 'Lord Hood' was fitted with 6ft. 3in. diameter coupled wheels – 4in. smaller than standard – for improved acceleration on steeply graded routes. These departures from standard specifications were found to be unjustified in everyday operation, although the locomotives concerned retained the features. The straightforward boiler and Belpaire firebox (the latter of record dimensions for the S.R. at the time, giving rise to all but non-stop work for the fireman) were discarded on No.857 'Lord Howe' in favour of a much enlarged boiler constructed to the limits of the loading gauge, in combination with a round-topped firebox, which were prepared in accordance with dimensions from Maunsell's Pacific project. Fruitless though the investigation of the boiler's propensities were in view of the stillborn nature of the proposal, No.857 nevertheless reverted to standard only when the boiler finally passed beyond reasonable repair many years later.

Smoke deflectors were applied to the entire class in the early 1930s, which heightened the already impressive stance of the class, and the 4,000-gallon bogie tenders were eventually given added coal-carrying capacity by virtue of raised side sheets, of which the upper sections were canted inwards to clear the loading gauge. The sheer bulk of the 4-6-0s belied their comparatively low weight, little more than that of the 'King Arthurs', achieved by assiduous paring of excess metal and the use of high-tensile steel for valve gears and reciprocating parts.

Following a revitalised career, courtesy of Bulleid's successful modifications which vindicated their earlier promise, the magnificent 4-6-0s were consigned to the scrap heap in 1961-62. Appropriately the prototype, No.850 'Lord Nelson', has been salvaged by B.R. for preservation.

The latent power evoked by the excellent proportions of Maunsell's largest product is amply portrayed by No.30860 'Lord Hawke', captured alongside Eastleigh works in April 1958. Note the high-sided tender and wide Bulleid chimney. (F. Hornby)

MAUNSELL 'LORD NELSON' CLASS 4-6-0, 1926

MAUNSELL 'LORD NELSON' CLASS 4-6-0, 1926

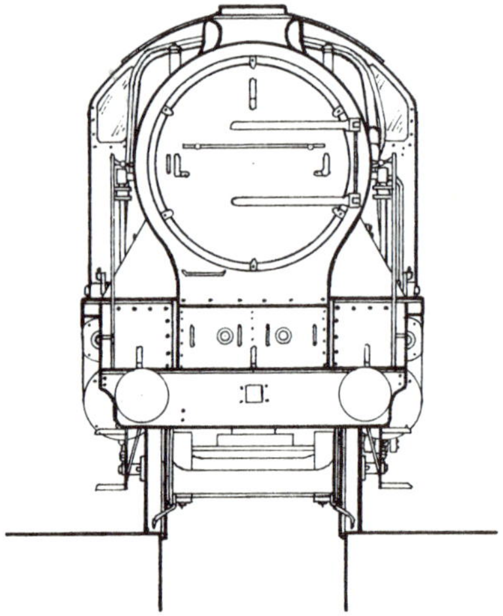

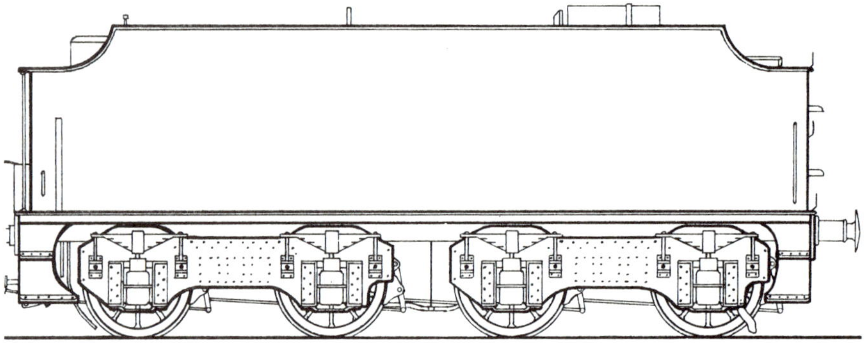

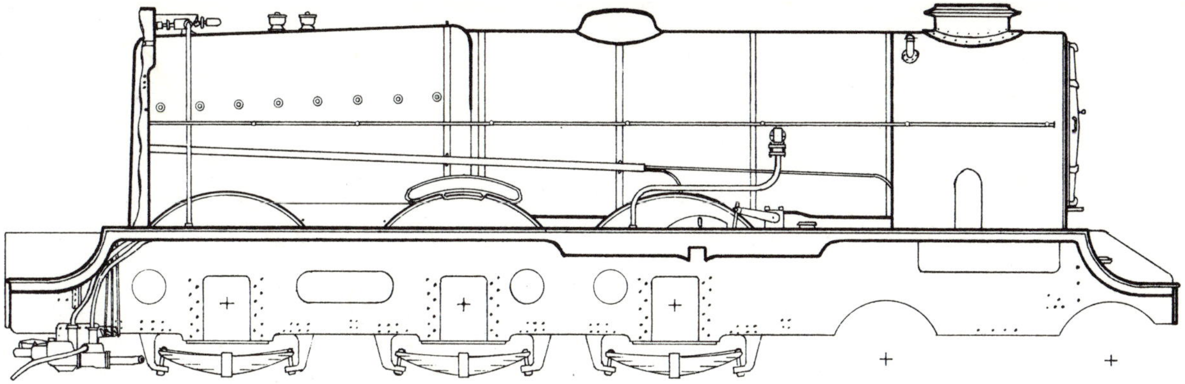

FRAME DETAILS, BULLEID CHIMNEY, AND EXHAUST STEAM INJECTOR. SMOKE DEFLECTORS NOT SHOWN

MAUNSELL 'LORD NELSON' CLASS 4-6-0, 1926

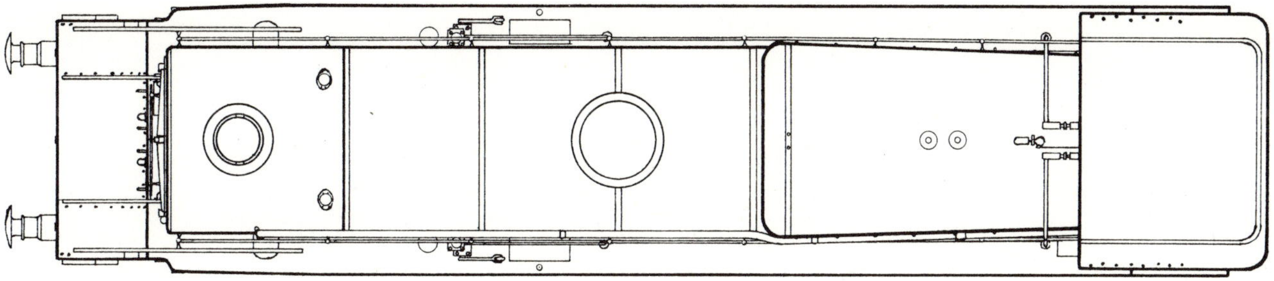

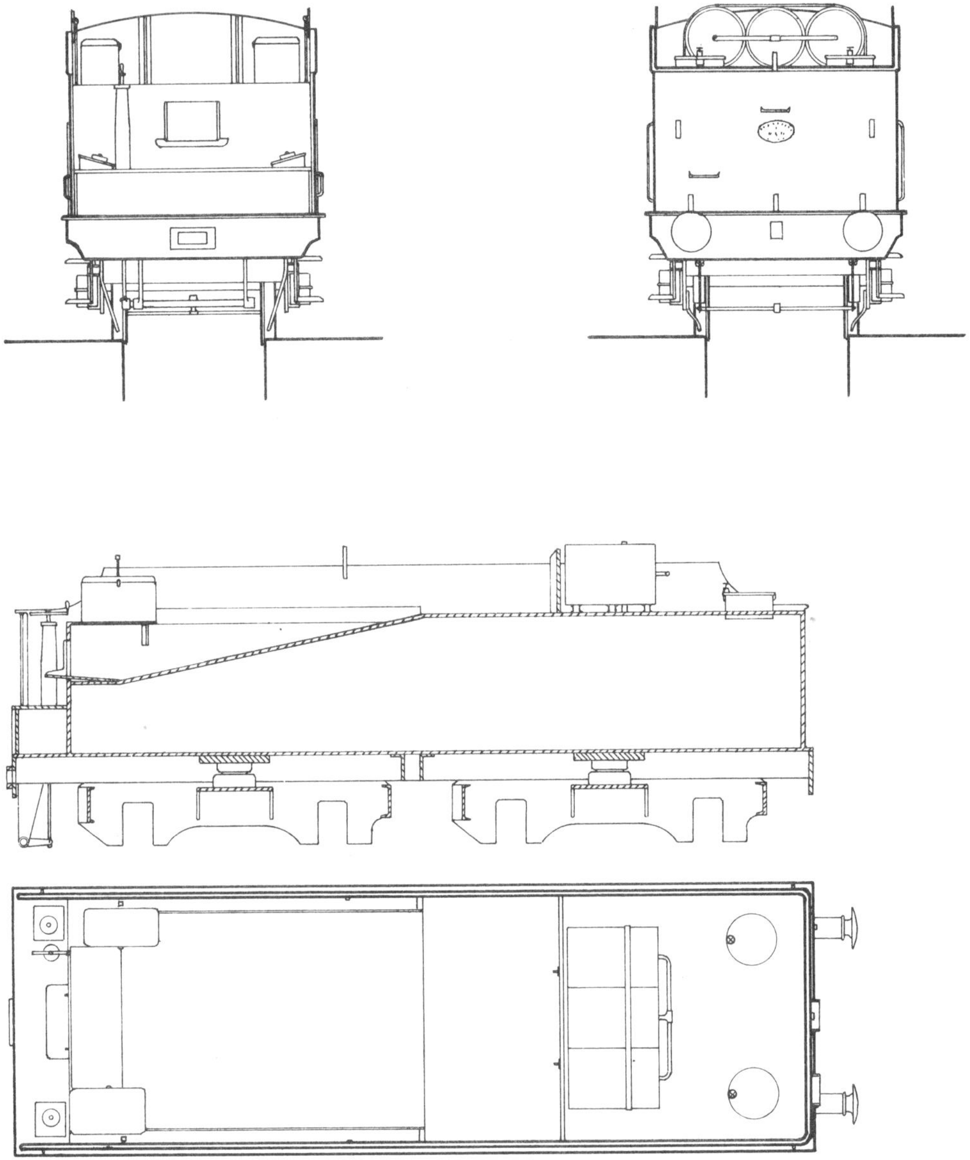

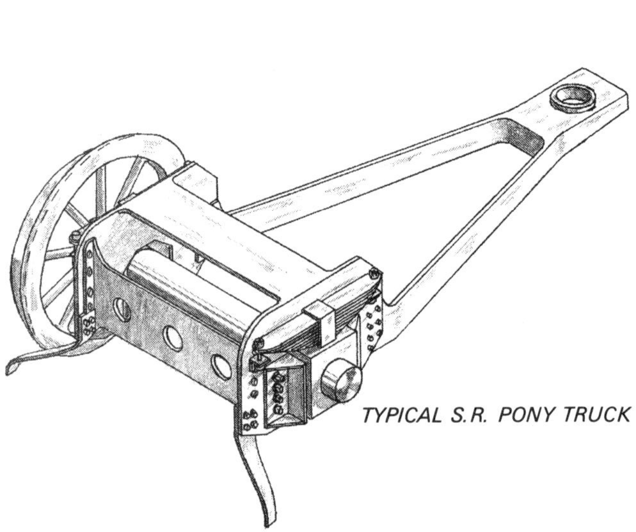

TYPICAL S.R. PONY TRUCK

MAUNSELL 'LORD NELSON' CLASS 4-6-0, 1926

Basically similar to and developed from the N Class Moguls with which many parts were interchangeable, the larger-wheeled U Class 2-6-0s were advocated in the late 1920s in answer to demands from the running department for a tender-locomotive fleet to supplement the K or 'River' Class tank locomotives, whose water-carrying capacity was necessarily limited, on medium passenger traffic. The heavy 2-6-4 tanks were themselves direct counterparts of the N Class engines, having been launched in the same year (1917), and further examples additional to the twenty-strong fleet were commissioned simultaneously with the U Moguls; however, a series of minor excursions off the road culminating in a serious high-speed derailment involving No.800 'River Cray' at Sevenoaks in August 1927, in which thirteen people lost their lives, caused the entire class of 2-6-4Ts to be withdrawn from service pending thorough examination. Although the design was eventually exonerated, via the good offices of Nigel Gresley in conducting rigorous trials on the superbly maintained L.N.E.R. tracks, the S.R. authorities considered that since the general state of Southern permanent way nowhere matched the excellence of the L.N.E.R., large tank locomotives were to be totally banned from the system. None were built thereafter, apart from two small batches of specialised freight and shunting classes.

As a consequence of this directive, the engineering department was instructed to convert the twenty K Class engines into U Class tender format – a decision taken after the initial go-ahead for construction of U Class 2-6-0s, even though the first conversion from the 2-6-4Ts appeared three months before outshopping of the first 'scratch-built' Mogul in June 1928.

Fifty locomotives comprised the U Class in total, of which twenty were 'River' Class rebuilds (the nameplates were dropped) and the remaining thirty built from new between 1928 and 1931. All were equipped for righthand driving. A number of minor differences distinguished the rebuilds, chiefly in the region of the running plates, which were lower-set and surmounted by prominent wheel splashers, the latter fixtures on the 'scratch-built' versions being minute by comparison. In common with their N Class progenitors, the majority of U Class 2-6-0s were originally provided with piston tail rods, discarded during the 1930s. From 1933 onwards distinctive S.R. smoke deflectors were installed as each locomotive passed through the workshops on general overhaul. Six-wheel tenders of 3,500-gallon water capacity were initially supplied to most of the class; however, the release of these for use on Q Class 0-6-0s in 1938 involved replacement by larger-capacity tenders, featuring characteristic S.R. inward-curving top sections to the side panels.

Much excellent work was performed by the trustworthy U Moguls on the London-Portsmouth line, until the advent of the immensely competent 'Schools' 4-4-0s caused dispersal of many 2-6-0s into the more westerly reaches of the Western Section. Here the locomotives enjoyed popular and affectionate attention from their crews for the remainder of their career. Semi-fast passenger duties were frequently undertaken over the Eastern Section, although a gradual change in operational emphasis following cessation of hostilities in 1945 and particularly Nationalisation three years later – when widespread electrification of principal passenger routes forged apace – motivated reclassification of the U Class 2-6-0s as mixed traffic hauliers. This was a role to which they were entirely suited.

Beginning in the mid-1950s, approximately half the class were subjected to front-end modifications under the aegis of B.R., intended to enhance their inherently good steaming qualities. The imminence of withdrawal precipitated cancellation of further adaptations in 1961 and scrapping of the Moguls commenced two years later, with the last of the line relegated to the cutting torch in 1966. One U Class 2-6-0 has been rescued for posterity.

Formerly 2-6-4T No.804 'River Tamar' rebuilt in 1928, No.31804 is depicted resting at Eastleigh in March 1960.
(F. Hornby)

MAUNSELL U CLASS 2-6-0, 1928

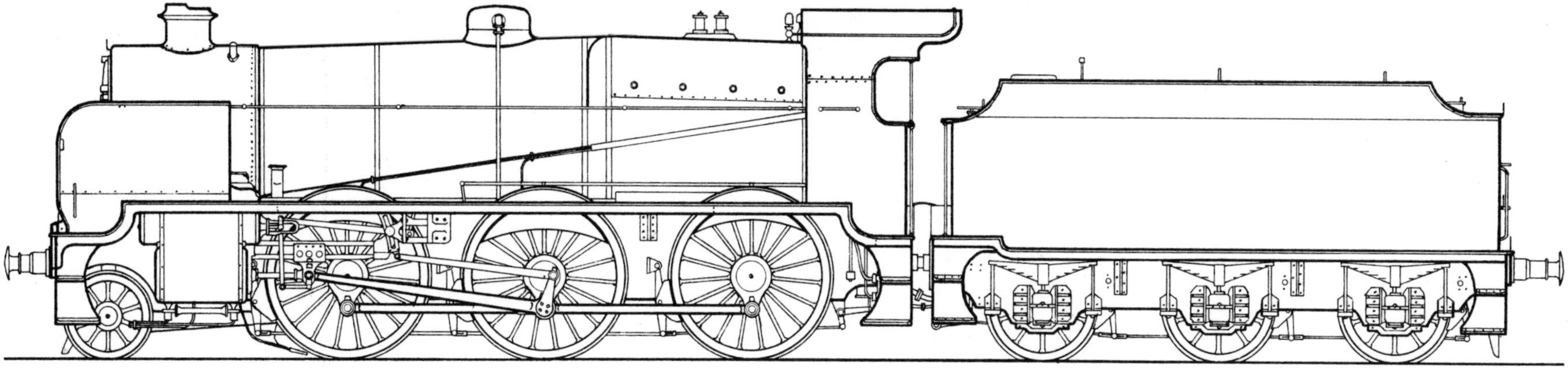

MAUNSELL U CLASS 2-6-0, 1928

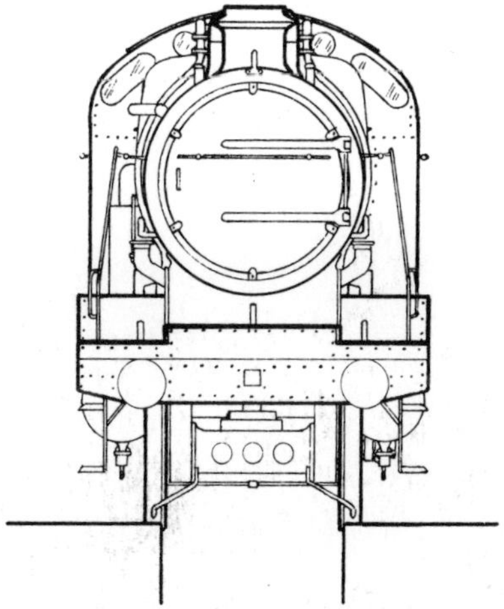

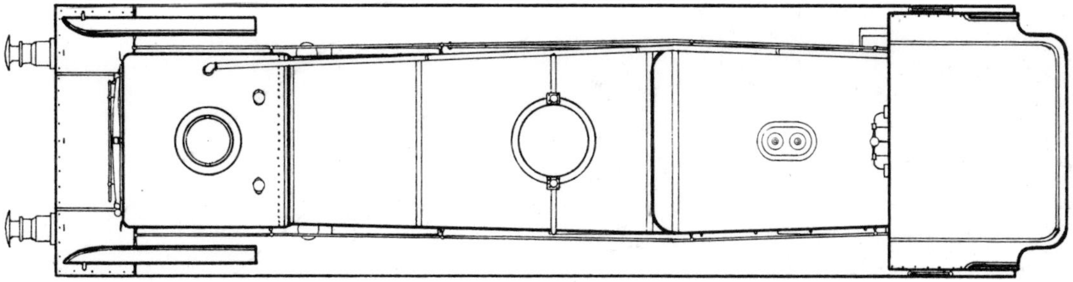

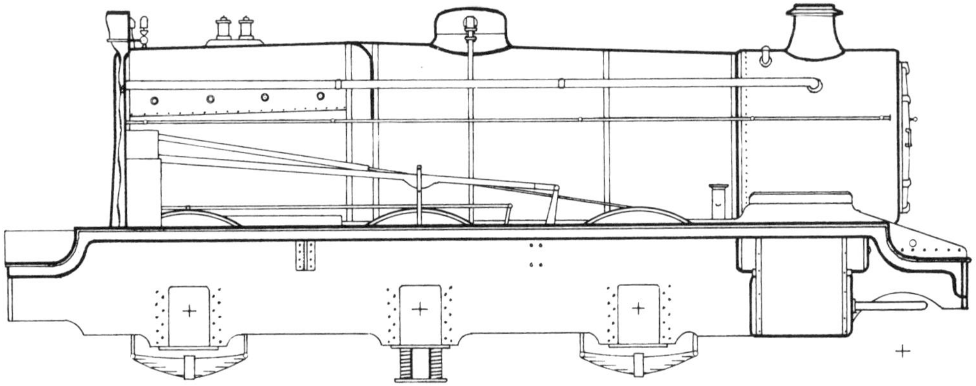

SHOWING REVERSE ROD AND BRAKE EJECTOR PIPE, PISTON TAIL ROD AND ORIGINAL TAPERED CHIMNEY. BASIC FRAME DETAILS ALSO COMMON TO U1 CLASS

U-Class 2-6-0 (two cylinder)

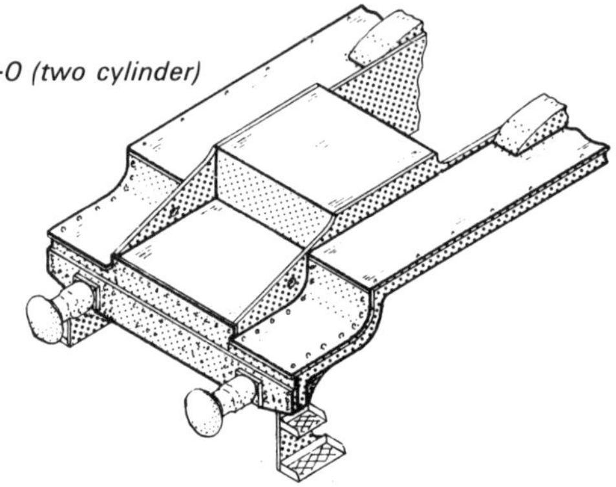

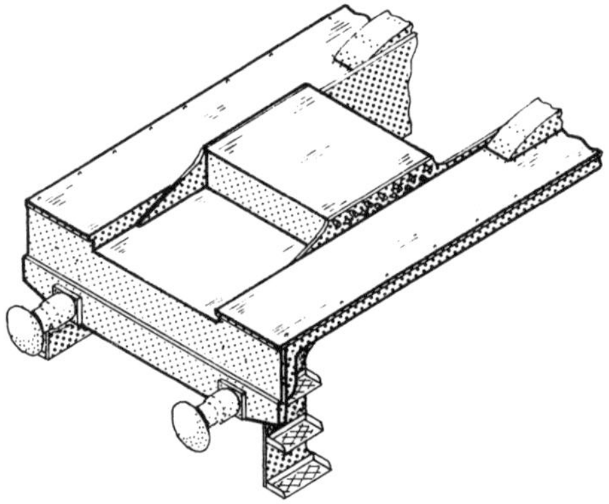

U1-Class 2-6-0 (three cylinder)
Buffer beam and front running-plate raised to clear central cylinder

MAUNSELL U CLASS 2-6-0, 1928

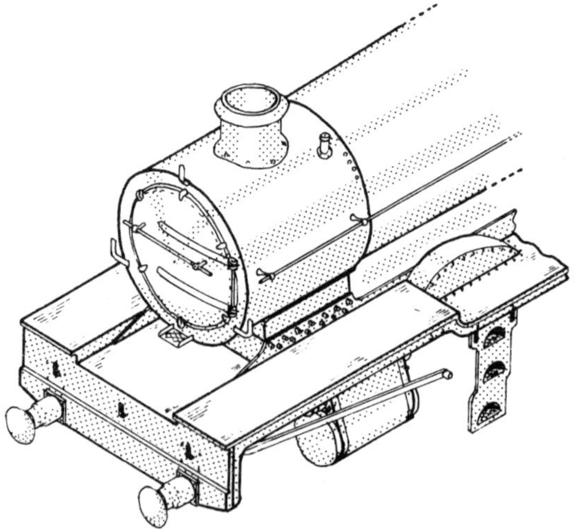

Prototype U1 No.890 in initial (1928) condition, retaining Holcroft conjugated valve gear (actuating rod to central cylinder shown) and steps of K1-Class 2-6-4T from which it was converted. Unique to No.890, running-plate stepped-down behind cylinder

Deployed on medium-fast passenger duties on the Eastern Section and the prestigious London-Portsmouth line – until displaced from the latter in the mid-1930s by 'Schools' 4-4-0s – alongside their U Class brethren, together with frequent spells of freight haulage for which the smooth power delivery imparted by their three-cylinder layout was eminently suitable, the speedy and accelerative U.1 Class 2-6-0s were prime movers of no mean versatility. The intense, heavily-laden traffic engendered by the needs of war between 1939 and 1945 evoked with a vengeance the opportunity to work the locomotives to the limit of their endurance, a challenge they survived with flying colours. Their relatively light weight and therefore wide route availability, including the ability to run over the notoriously restricted-gauge Hastings line (which was and remains routed through a succession of ultra-narrow tunnels, for passage through which specially-constructed rolling stock and purpose-built locomotives have been provided since inception in the mid-nineteenth century; considering the enormous capital outlay this course of action has involved over the years, not to say the complex train marshalling required, it seems astounding that the tunnels themselves have never been widened to accept standard stock), was a major factor in the U.1s' remarkable range of activity, not only in wartime but throughout their service.

The class was derived from the metamorphosis of a unique offshoot of the K Class 2-6-4T design. This locomotive, No.890 'River Frome', was a three-cylinder variant completed in 1925 in which Holcroft's conjugated motion actuated the valves of the central cylinder, via a system of linkages controlled by the outside-mounted Walschaerts valve gears. This method of operation had been previously explored on the pioneer N.1 derivative of the S.E.C.R. N Class two-cylinder 2-6-0s. As a result of the company's edict following the Sevenoaks accident, No.890, categorised K.1, was converted in 1928 into 2-6-0 tender guise along U Class lines but retaining three-cylinder propulsion. Before embarking on full-scale assembly of U.1s, Maunsell was compelled to abandon Holcroft's valve motion owing to immutable problems of over-running – that is, central valves running wildly out of sequence on trailing regulator – substituting a third set of time-proven Walschaerts motion. The prototype U.1 was thus modified in due course.

A production run of twenty U.1 Class 2-6-0s emerged from Eastleigh shops in 1931-32, differing externally from the precursive U Class (with which most parts were interchangeable) in possessing higher-set boilers (to allow adequate clearance for the central cylinder) and continuous horizontal running plates from cab to unusually deep buffer beams. By contrast, the initial U.1, No.890 – the ex-K.1 number was retained, less the name – sported running plates stepped down aft of the cylinders and thus located rather lower over the coupled wheels, combined with more voluminous wheel splashers.

In compliance with S.R. policy, smoke deflectors were affixed to the series in the mid-1930s, and after Nationalisation in 1948 the typical Maunsell superheater relief valves were deleted from the smokebox shells. Otherwise the locomotives continued to conform to original specification until withdrawal took place, excepting the application of new cylinders to a limited number during the 1950s. Scrapping of these highly successful locomotives was effected between 1962 and 1963, doomed without exception to extinction.

The penultimate member of the class, a recently-scrubbed No.31909 stands prepared for duty at Tonbridge shed in May 1957. Akin to the U Class locomotives, the 'dome' merely housed the top-feed mechanism and righthand drive was standard. (N.L. Browne)

MAUNSELL U1 CLASS 2-6-0, 1928

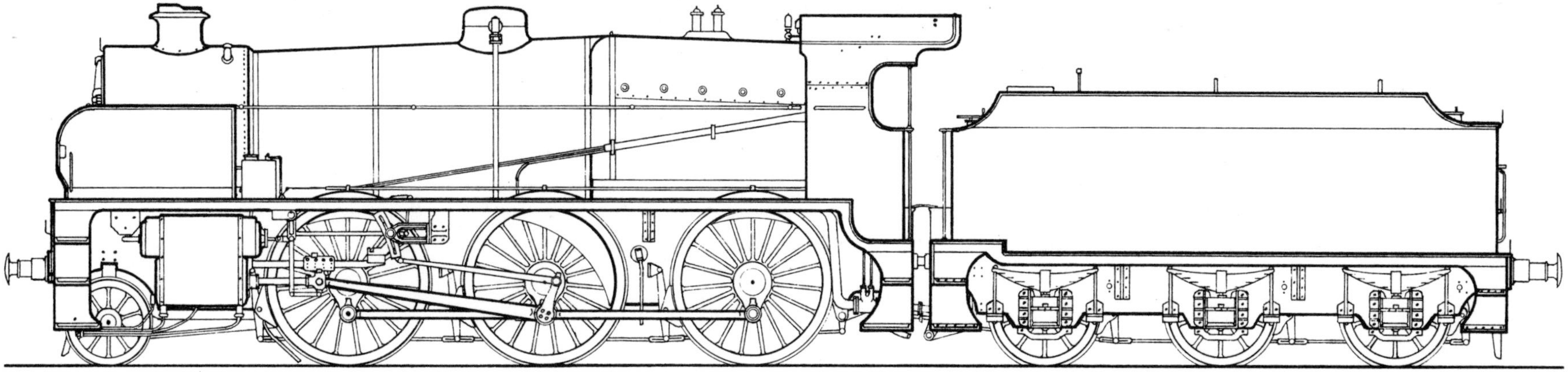

MAUNSELL U1 CLASS 2-6-0, 1928

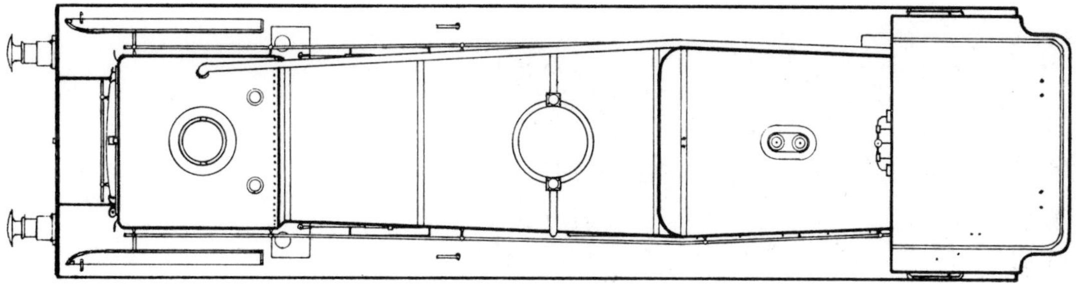

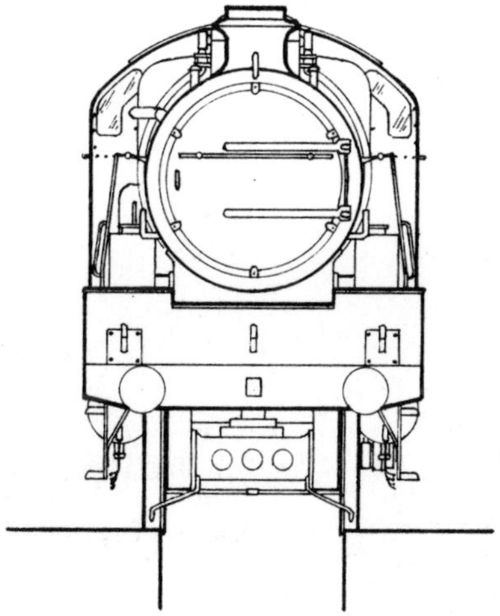

MAUNSELL Z CLASS 0-8-0T, 1929

In planning the counterparts to a class of 4-8-0Ts, instituted by Urie on the L.S.W.R. shortly before Grouping, Maunsell not only sought to procure the particular characteristics desirable in a shunting engine but also took into account the well-being of those people who happened to live adjacent to marshalling yards. In these inherently noisy places, the din of constant activity was significantly attributed to very hard-pressed locomotives.

Rather than perpetuate Urie's design, which naturally called for predominantly L.S.W.R-orientated parts, Maunsell opted for an entirely new blueprint utilising as many standard S.R. parts as possible, in conjunction with readily-available L.B.S.C.R.-type non-superheated boilers of large capacity and thereby able to retain steam pressure over prolonged periods without lifting the safety valves. This was one of the three criteria for a 'quiet' locomotive, the other two being a muted exhaust, and good adhesion to avoid slipping. The second desideratum was successfully incorporated, and the third was ensured by use of three U.1 Class cylinders linked to divided drive (the central cylinder drove the second axle, the outside cylinders the third) in order to spread the innately smooth power delivery more equably over the eight small-diameter coupled wheels. The adhesion factor was additionally improved by concentration of the full engine weight of 71½ tons on the coupled wheels alone, by virtue of the lack of leading or trailing pony trucks. A measure of side-play was built into the first and fourth axles to permit a stipulated manoeuvrability around curves of 4½-chain minimum radius.

Externally the Z Class 0-8-0Ts were unique. Stubby side-mounted water tanks incorporating sloped upper surfaces for good crew vision, smokeboxes of smaller diameter than the abutting boilers and elevated running plates over the prominent outside cylinders gave the locomotives a flavour all their own. Eight examples were outshopped from Brighton in 1929 and were sent to various yards within the S.R. empire. Quickly establishing a reputation for high but easily manageable power output, the bulky tanks were well-regarded by their crews – and popular with yard-side residents. Sanction for ten more was obtained in 1931, but severe economies forced on the S.R. by the onset and protracted effect of the Great Depression caused termination of the order before construction had started: the class strength therefore remained static at eight.

During World War II six Z Class locomotives were temporarily removed to Scotland on loan to the War Department – their reputation for reliability and surefooted vigour preceded them – whereas under B.R. direction the class was assigned to broader spheres of operation than that for which the design had been propounded. Occasional bouts of heavy freight haulage, albeit over short distances due to restricted water-carrying capacity and attainable speed, were ably undertaken and latterly several 0-8-0Ts were allocated onto banking and pilot duties. Two such locomotives were shedded at Exeter, having displaced a handful of venerable ex-L.B.S.C.R. E1R Class 0-6-2Ts on the short but steeply graded (1 in 37) connecting line between G.W.R./S.R.-joint St. Davids and S.R. Central (ex-Queen Street) stations. It was quite normal to witness both Z Class tanks assisting a single train up this vicious incline.

The eight constituents of the Z Class were despatched to the scrapyards in 1962.

This shot of No.30951 sandwiched between B.R. Standard locomotives at Ashford shed in May 1958 convincingly illustrates the brute power of the massive S.R. shunters.
(F. Hornby)

MAUNSELL Z CLASS 0-8-0T, 1929

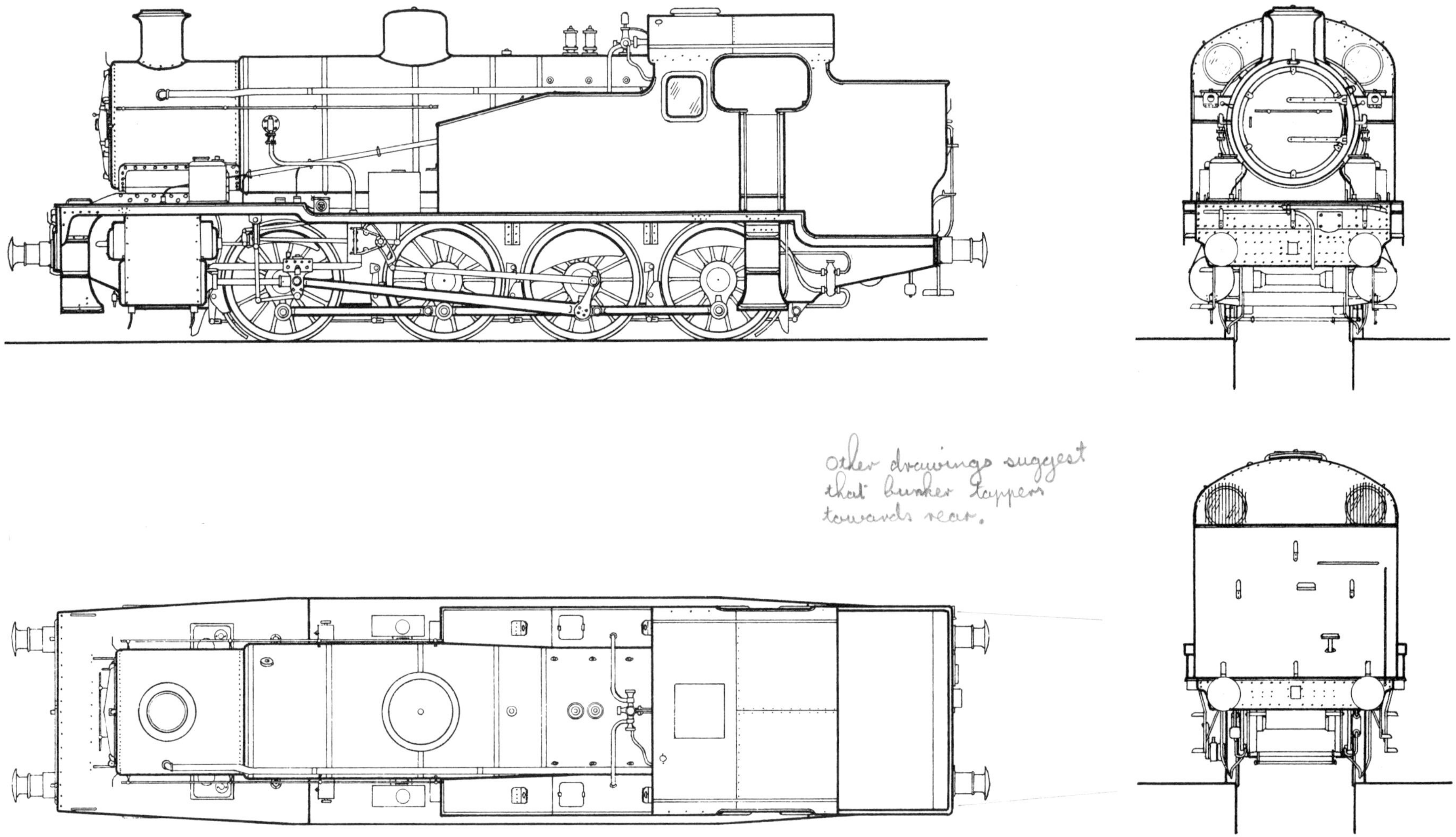

MAUNSELL Z CLASS 0-8-0T, 1929

Maunsell's last and finest express design to be built for the S.R., the outstandingly successful 'Schools' 4-4-0, was the C.M.E.'s response to pressure from the traffic department for a medium-fast passenger design along the lines of the 'Lord Nelson' 4-6-0s, but having a wider route availability together with similar power characteristics to the 'King Arthur' series. The upshot proved not only the final, most powerful express in the celebrated tradition of British 4-4-0 steam locomotives but was also claimed to be the most powerful of its type in Europe.

Bearing in mind the proviso that the outcome would be allocated to the restricted-gauge Hastings line, amongst other destinations, Maunsell adapted the 'King Arthur' boiler pattern in preference to the more modern 'Lord Nelson' version. This was due to the fact that the Belpaire firebox of the latter would gravely interfere with forward vision from the necessarily constricted cab, whereas the round-topped firebox of the earlier 4-6-0s allowed a reasonable degree of vision from a cab whose sidesheets had to be canted inwards approximately midway up their height for clearance of the Hastings gauge. 'Lord Nelson' wheels, cylinders, reciprocating and valve motion were chosen for the three-cylinder configuration, so that by using many standard S.R. parts Maunsell achieved a comparatively inexpensive locomotive.

Altogether forty V Class (the official nomenclature) 4-4-0s were assembled, the initial ten in 1930 and the remaining thirty between 1932 and 1935. Of these, all but the 1930 batch were equipped from new with smoke deflectors; the original engines were so fitted by the close of the overall construction programme in 1935. The ever-alert S.R. public relations office coined the notion of naming the locomotives for well-known public schools and, in a brilliant publicity campaign, arranged as far as possible for each individual engine to be viewed and inspected by the boys attending the foundation it commemorated.

The prowess of the class rapidly came to the fore on taking over the London-Portsmouth express services from U and U.1 Class 2-6-0s, amongst others, in conjunction with a great deal of seemingly effortless working on the heavier passenger traffic over Eastern Section lines. So overwhelmingly successful were the 'Schools' at the exploitation of arduous duties that in 1938 they superseded the much larger 'King Arthurs' on the crack London-Portsmouth trains, on which their staggering level of performance reinforced beyond doubt the general opinion that Maunsell had indeed produced a masterpiece in steam technology.

Shortly before the outbreak of World War II, Bulleid experimentally applied his modified Lemaitre system of multiple-blast pipes and wide chimney to a number of 'Schools'. However, unlike the transformation wrought on the 'Lord Nelsons', the steaming quality of the 4-4-0s, already excellent, was not drastically affected and only 21 members of the class were adapted in this way. Bulleid's theories on streamlining, eventually to materialise on his Pacifics of the 1940s, took the form of a full-scale mock-up enshrouding the boiler of a 'Schools' locomotive; the imminence of war and its consequences in the autumn of 1939 prevented progressive development on this fascinating 4-4-0 theme.

In B.R. days the 4-4-0s continued to dominate the Eastern Section express operation, most especially on the Hastings route, until the tide of dieselisation washed over the class. Towards the end of the steam era, several 'Schools' were allocated to haulage of Royal trains –an appropriate honour – for which purpose the engines involved were maintained in sparkling condition.

Withdrawal of the 'Schools' arrived relatively early, the B.R. policy of locomotive re-equipment for Southern Region tending to concentrate on passenger services as a priority. Thus the forty Maunsell 4-4-0s vanished in 1961 and 1962. Three have been preserved, of which one now resides in the United States.

A few were fitted with Lord Nelson tenders after the withdrawal of that class.

The elegance and substantial power of the big 4-4-0s is underscored by No.30910 'Merchant Taylors' in steam at Newhaven in April 1958. Note the 'single' chimney, standard 4,000-gallon tender and neat splashguard over the rear bogie wheel.

(F. Hornby)

MAUNSELL V CLASS 'SCHOOLS' 4-4-0, 1930

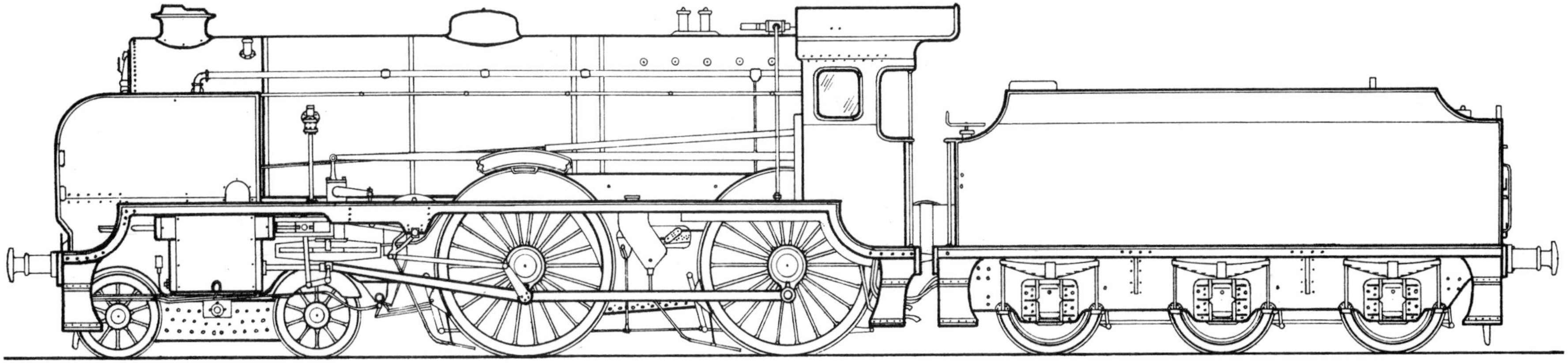

MAUNSELL V CLASS 'SCHOOLS' 4-4-0, 1930

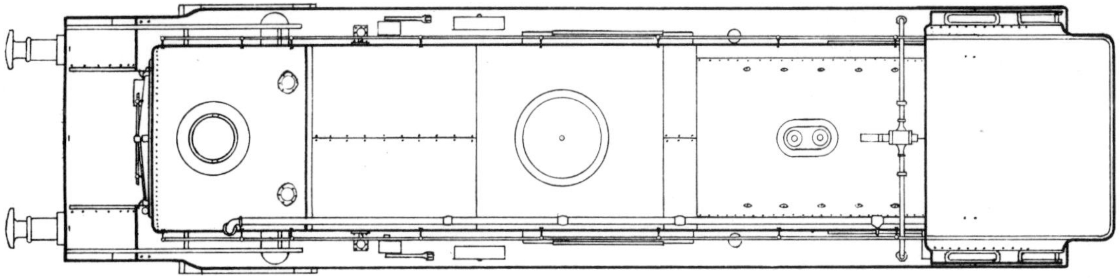

MAUNSELL V CLASS 'SCHOOLS' 4-4-0, 1930

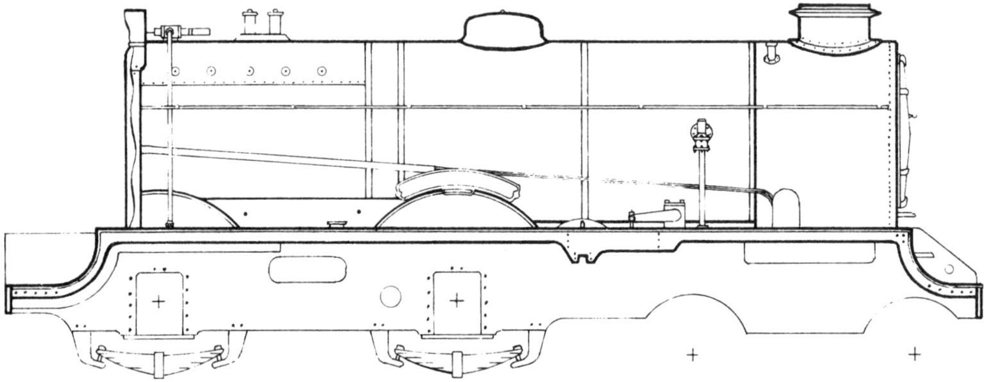

LESS DEFLECTORS, SHOWING FRAME DETAIL AND BULLEID CHIMNEY

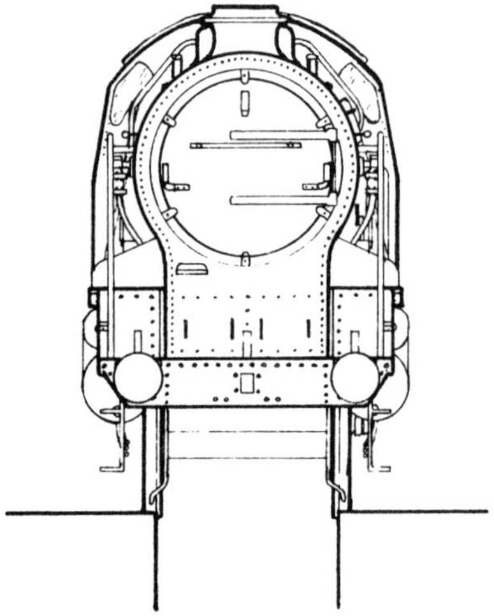

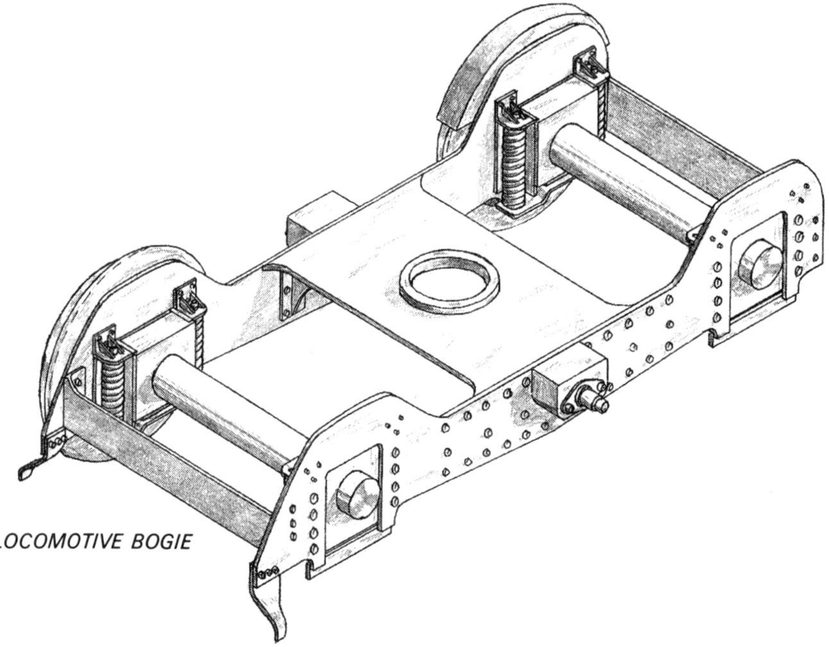

TYPICAL S.R. LOCOMOTIVE BOGIE

In spite of the permanent ban on heavy tank locomotives for passenger transportation, the use of such engines for freight traffic over short distances and in conditions where sustained high speed was unattainable was favourably viewed by the S.R. directors, when Maunsell formulated a three-cylinder 2-6-4T proposition for work in the London area. The board inclined further towards the C.M.E.'s notion on inspecting the design specification, by virtue of the incorporation of standard items such as U.1 cylinders, motion and boilers, N Class coupled wheels and pony trucks, together with numerous articles held in store from the dismantled 'River' Class 2-6-4Ts including side tanks and bogies. This produced not only a financially viable design but also one of well-proven characteristics.

The movement of freight around the Capital was a fairly low-key but nonetheless important side of S.R. business activities; since goods trains had to be interlinked with the immensely complicated daily suburban passenger schedules, the locomotives employed thereon needed considerable power and acceleration; no time was allowable for turning purposes, so that more often than not engines ran tender-first – a potentially dangerous procedure on such densely-signalled lines. This latter was a primary motive for substituting tank locomotives capable of running with equal facility in either direction without loss of adequate crew vision.

Fifteen examples filled the W Class in a building programme lasting from 1931 to 1936, of which the initial five were rigged for righthand drive in the S.E.C.R. custom, the remainder driven from the left-hand side of the cab. Strangely, the righthand drive versions were outshopped from the Eastleigh works of the former L.H.D.-orientated L.S.W.R. whereas the later, L.H.D., engines hailed from the ex-S.E.C.R. shops at Ashford.

Three-cylinder propulsion was installed to provide the essential power and acceleration qualities; the central cylinder was controlled via a simple form of conjugated motion actuated by the outside Walschaerts gear sets. A sophisticated method of valve actuation was strictly superfluous on both operational and monetary grounds, since the locomotives evinced the low attainable speeds commensurate with goods working.

The massive 2-6-4Ts featured a very rare fitment on post-Edwardian steam designs, a braking system for the bogie wheels in addition to the conventional coupled wheel brakes, since the profusion of gradients and short block sections (i.e., involving continual halting at adverse signals) in the sphere of operation demanded above-average stopping power.

The highly successful W Class tanks eked out their entire service lives on the duties and in the region for which they had been created. The prospect of disbandment became a reality in 1963-64, when the fleet was discarded in favour of diesel-powered units.

Strongly resembling the former K Class 2-6-4Ts, a grimy W Class engine No.31925 stands cold and forlorn at Eastleigh sheds upon withdrawal in November 1963.
(F. Hornby)

MAUNSELL W CLASS 2-6-4T, 1931

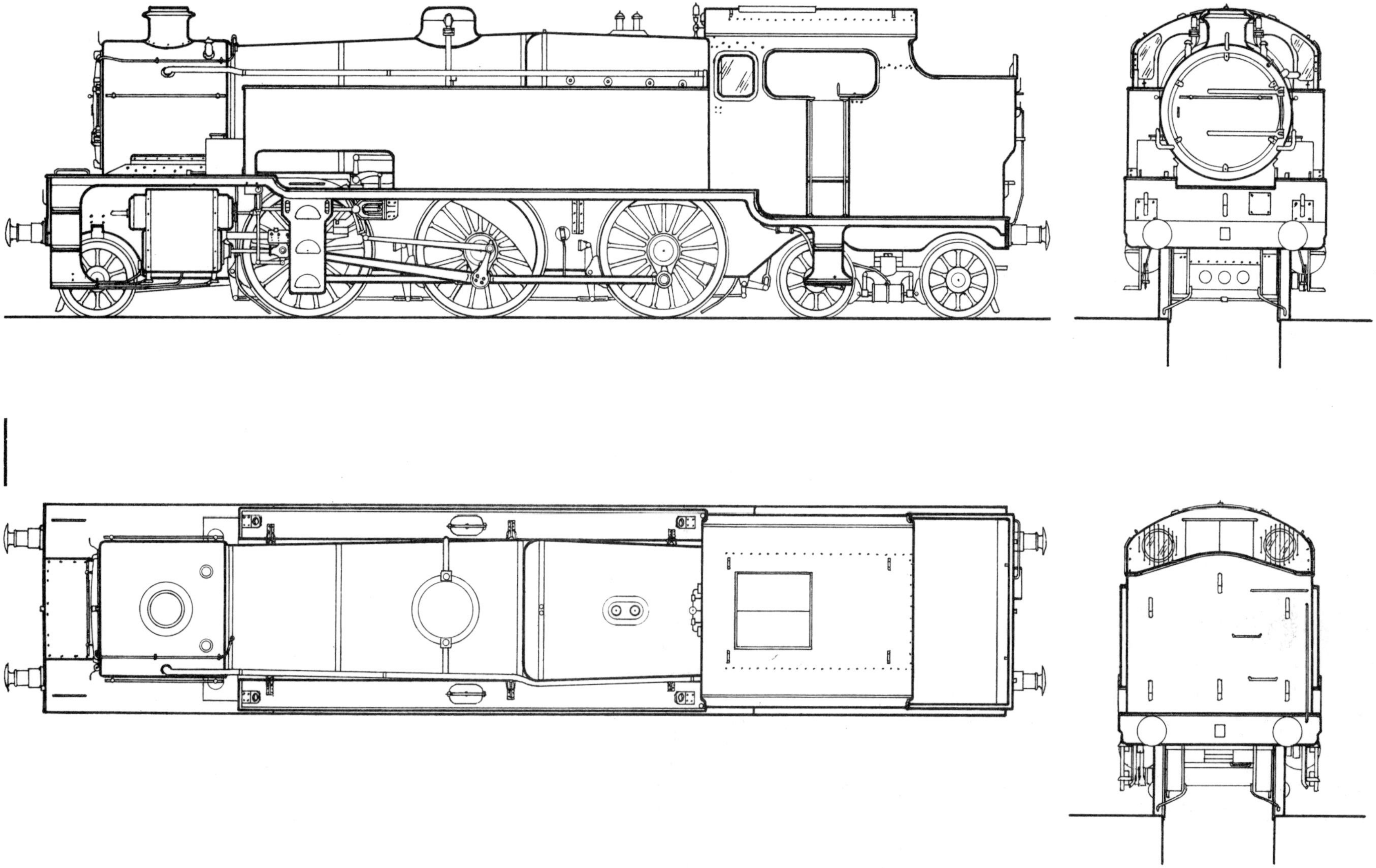

MAUNSELL W CLASS 2-6-4T, 1931

MAUNSELL N15x CLASS 4-6-0, 1934

The rigid prohibition enforced against large passenger tank locomotives from the late 1920s onwards gradually filtered down the roster of affected motive power stock inherited from the constituent main line railways. Amongst these was a small but elite collection of seven celebrated 4-6-4Ts, built to Lawson Billinton's design by the L.B.S.C.R. between 1914 and 1922. These had performed some stupendous feats of speed and endurance on the Eastbourne and Brighton lines for which they had been mooted, until electrification of their stamping grounds in the early 1930s eliminated their primary function.

Ranking amongst the mightiest of all British tank locomotives, the magnificent Baltics were the undoubted flagships of the L.B.S.C.R. fleet. While subjected to a number of early riding problems that were effectively ironed out before the advent of Grouping, the overall design was immensely successful and merited a much extended career in active service. The S.R. tank engine policy unfortunately countenanced no exceptions, however grandiloquent the characteristics of any pertinent class, and thus between 1934 and 1936 the seven 4-6-4Ts were converted into 4-6-0 tender locomotives, in which guise they retained considerable aesthetic panache but, notwithstanding the provision of upgraded boiler pressures and reworked cylinders, lost the crisp performance of the Billinton originals.

Never actively publicised to the degree accorded to the unadulterated Maunsell designs, the class acquired its familiar title 'Remembrance' on the basis that one of the Baltics was the L.B.S.C.R. 'war memorial locomotive' – the designation of an engine to honour the death in action of employees being a general practice amongst senior railway companies following World War I – its name and commemoration plates being transferred to the rebuild. Only three of the 4-6-4Ts had carried individual names, two of which were applied to the conversions; eventually the remaining five N15x (company classification) 4-6-0s were given names of leading nineteenth century locomotive engineers, inspired by Baltic No.2329 'Stephenson'.

Assigned to the London-Southampton passenger services, the reincarnated locomotives were in truth merely mediocre in their revised role; the 'King Arthur' 4-6-0s were much more spirited in comparison and were preferred by the crews, though they lacked the sheer power of their stablemates. During World War II a number of the 'Remembrance' Class were temporarily transferred to the G.W.R. for freight handling purposes; however, the situation obtaining on return to normality in 1945 on the S.R. and subsequent B.R. Southern Region, when Bulleid's Pacifics came to the fore, rendered the class largely superfluous to requirements. Dismemberment commenced in 1955, the final survivor – No.32331 'Beattie' – lingering on into 1957.

In conclusion, the rebuilt 4-6-0s were but pale shadows of the former all-conquering 4-6-4Ts. That such a conversion was imposed upon the class was a sad waste of an outstandingly accomplished design. Nevertheless the outcome of the uncompromising S.R. directive was certainly an impressive locomotive, in appearance if not in operation.

A fine portrait of an N15x locomotive, complete with standard 5,000-gallon bogie tender, No.32330 'Cudworth' pauses in steam at Clapham Junction in 1954.
(N.L. Browne)

MAUNSELL N15x CLASS 4-6-0, 1934

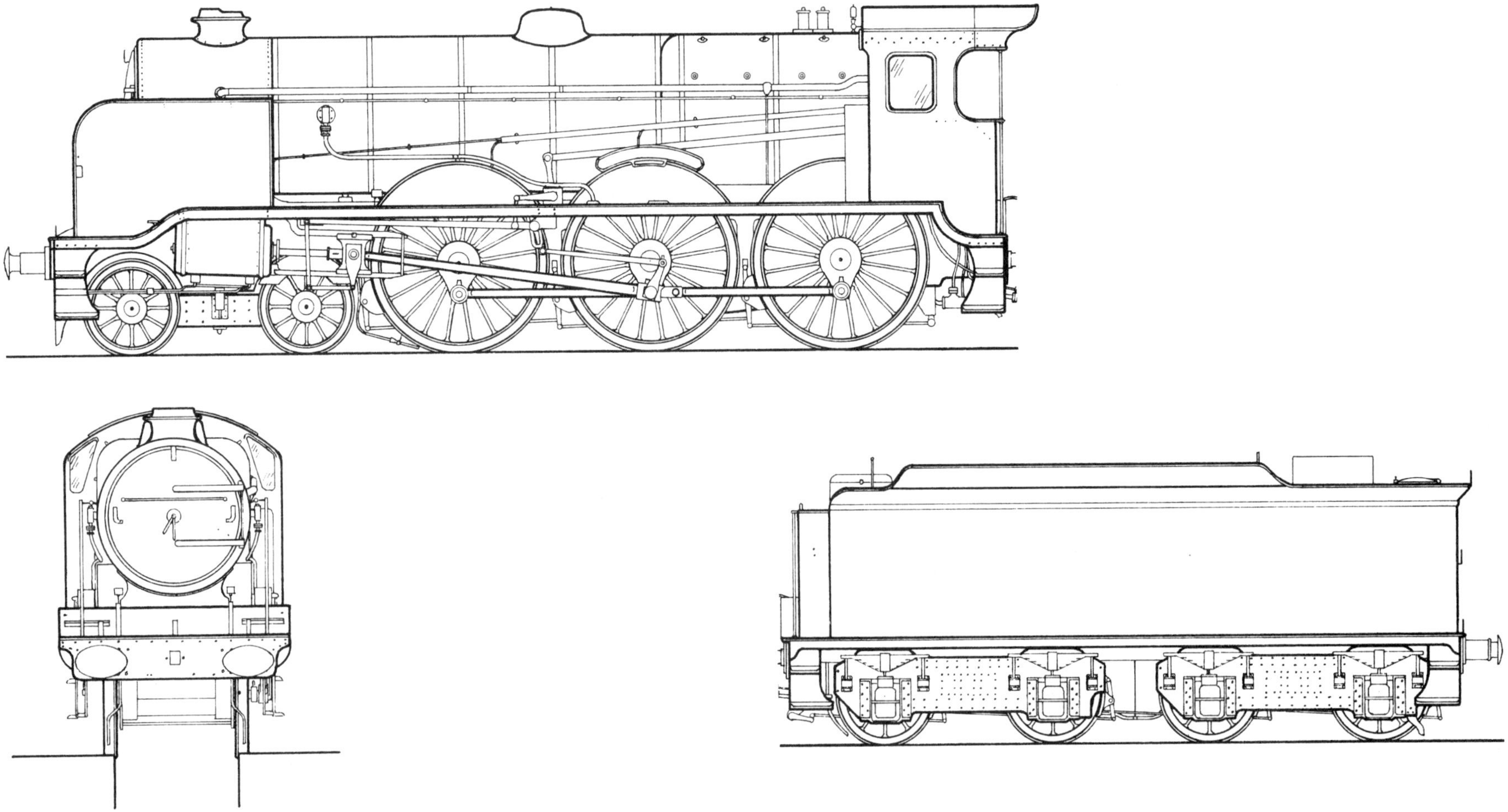

MAUNSELL N15x CLASS 4-6-0, 1934

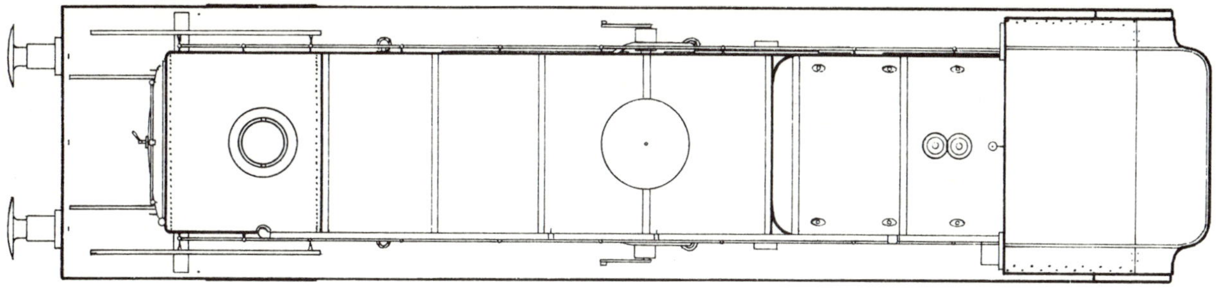

MAUNSELL N15x CLASS 4-6-0, 1934

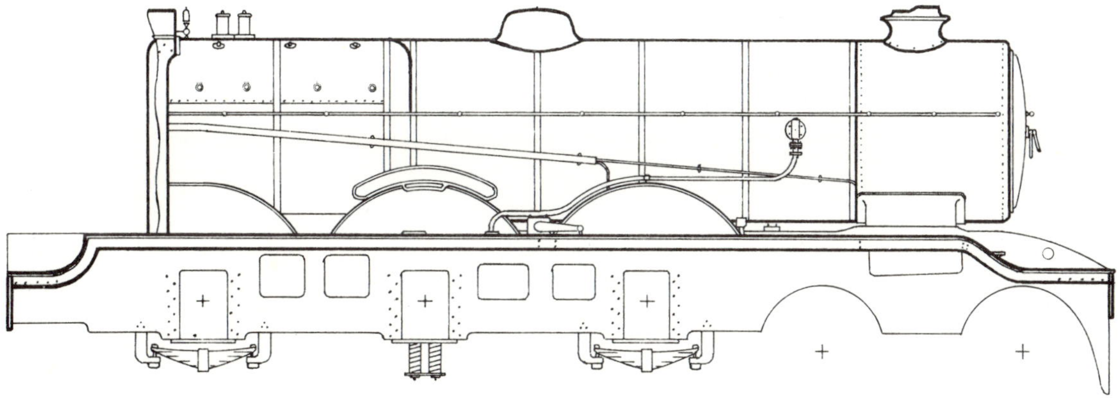

MINUS SMOKE DEFLECTORS, SHOWING FRAME DETAILS, SMOKEBOX SADDLE AND FIREBOX BACKPLATE

MAUNSELL Q CLASS 0-6-0, 1938

Primarily formulated for goods haulage over minor routes and branch lines, yet equipped for passenger working when required, the twenty Q Class locomotives comprised the first of only two indigenous S.R. 0-6-0 series and the last design from Maunsell's hand before his retirement. In replacing a variety of ancient hauliers – the majority of nineteenth century L.S.W.R. provenance – that had been maintained far beyond normal life expectancy owing to the dearth of more modern equivalents, the 0-6-0s were necessarily lightweight machines enabling negotiation of the worst-laid, most remote tracks in the S.R. network. They were therefore available for the widest possible range of routes – barring dockyards, the internal working of which called for locomotives of a specialised nature.

Although their archetypal 'British 0-6-0' appearance and unadventurous mechanical specification provoked the non-conformist Bulleid, under whose supremacy the engines were manufactured in 1938-39, into commenting wryly that had he 'arrived on the scene earlier, he would have prevented their building', the Qs were admirably suited to their allotted tasks and proved a considerable asset in the less exalted dominions within the Southern empire.

Complete with twin inside cylinders and Stephenson's link motion in the classic pattern, the 0-6-0 class was fitted with many standard S.R. parts in the interest of low capital expenditure. A fairly unusual feature was the use of steam reversing gear, more often than not a troublesome application but in this instance singularly reliable, evolved from that employed on a number of S.E.C.R. classes in late-Victorian and Edwardian times. All twenty locomotives were constructed for lefthand driving.

In common with the 'Lord Nelson' and 'Schools' designs, the humble Q Class 0-6-0s were selected for experimental modification via Bulleid's multi-jet blast pipe arrangements. Several were thus fitted and demonstrated a perceptibly improved power output; however, the cost of such fitments did not merit installation over the whole class. It was left to B.R. to conduct further blast pipe experiments in the 1950s, with generally desultory results.

Maunsell's willing workhorses of the minor lines were consigned to the breakers' yards between 1962 and 1965, without preservation.

An unmistakably British 0-6-0 design, Q Class No.30530 – first of the twenty outshopped – simmers gently at Eastleigh shed in August 1963. (F. Hornby)

MAUNSELL Q CLASS 0-6-0, 1938

48

MAUNSELL Q CLASS 0-6-0, 1938

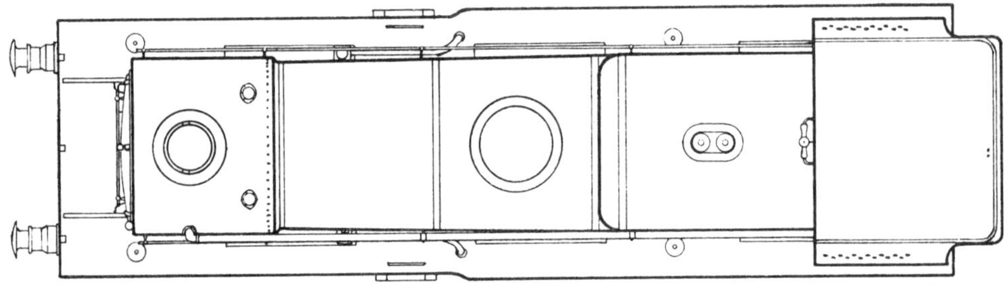

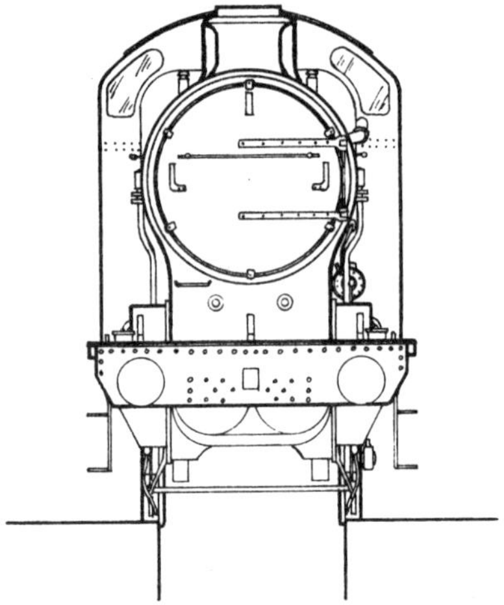

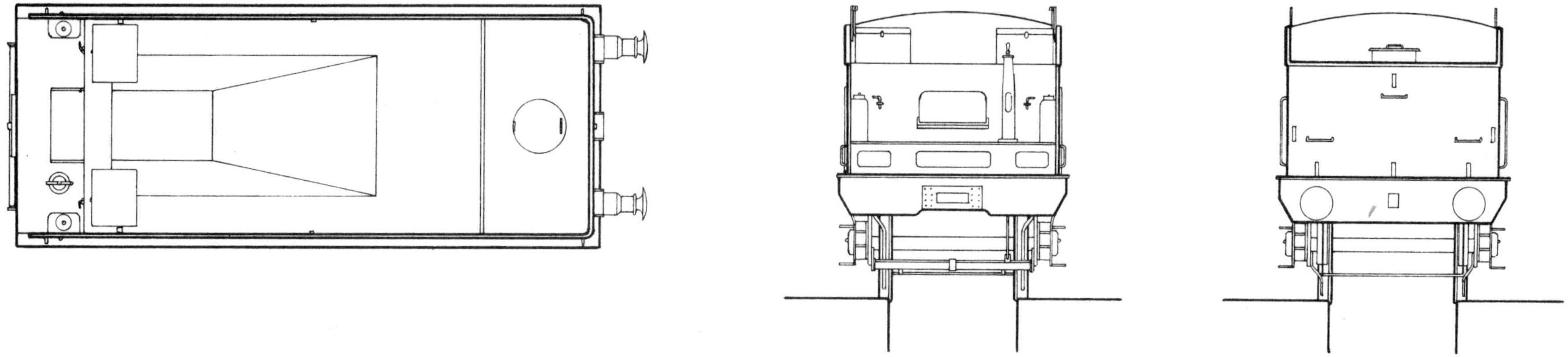

3500-GALLON TENDER, AS FITTED TO Q CLASS 0-6-0

MAUNSELL Q CLASS 0-6-0, 1938

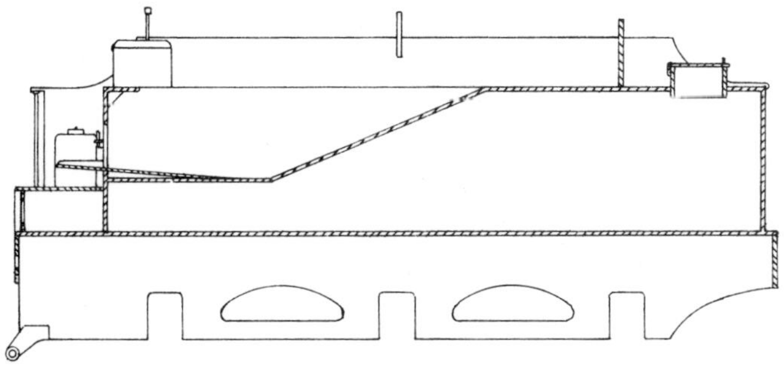

BULLEID-LEMAÎTRE MULTI-JET BLAST PIPE SYSTEM
(Shown fitted to Q-Class 0-6-0 locomotive)
Arrangement comprises five radially-disposed blast nozzles, exhausting through large-diameter chimney

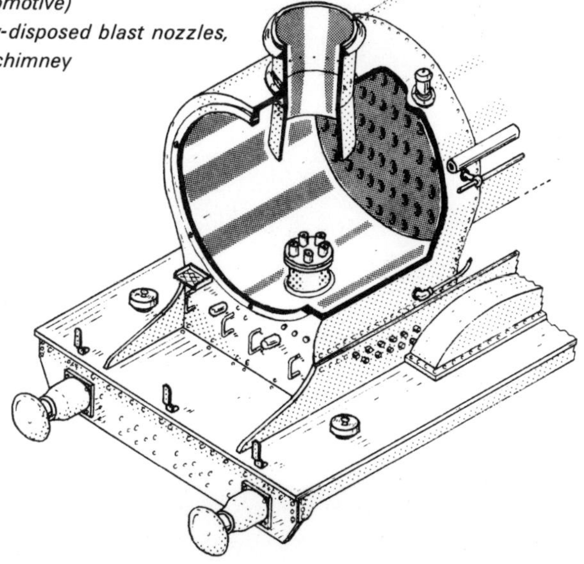

The reception accorded to O.V.S. Bulleid's radical Q.1 Class 0-6-0 on its unveiling in 1942 was a splendid mixture of astonishment, disbelief and contempt. Never one to swim with the tide, Bulleid revelled in the howls of horror from his contemporaries, knowing that he had created a locomotive of unequalled power for its size and wheel arrangement.

The emphasis away from passenger transportation to freight haulage during World War II found the S.R. at a distinct disadvantage compared with the other three Groups: the paucity of pure goods locomotives was keenly felt, so that the Government – at that time in control of railway management – sanctioned the building of forty suitable 0-6-0s for the company. Bulleid is on record as explaining that an expansion of Maunsell's Q Class would have proved the easiest course to adopt, except that that design was not fully able to handle the massive burdens imposed by the war effort.

Twin inside cylinders (of improved format), Stephenson's link motion and Q Class brakes were retained, but modified 'Lord Nelson' Belpaire fireboxes were installed in conjunction with tapered boilers; smokeboxes contained Bulleid's Lemaître-type multiple-blast pipes. In successfully accomplishing the demand for high tractive effort with lowest possible axle load in concert with the wartime strictures in supply of steel, Bulleid cast aside running plates and wheel splashers, utilised Bulleid-Firth-Brown Boxpok wheels (lighter and giving more uniform support for tyres than conventional spoked wheels) first introduced on the 'Merchant Navy' 4-6-2s in 1941, and clad the boiler/firebox combination – which met express passenger standards – in ultra-distinctive, thin steel sheeting supported by the main frames.

The bizarre appearance of the Q.1s, alternatively known as 'Austerity' 0-6-0s, was functional in the extreme. All concessions to the merest hint of traditional elegance were dispensed with, and to most enthusiasts the class will always be regarded as the most grotesque ever to roll on British rails. Nevertheless, in some – perhaps more perverse – eyes the engine exhibits a stark, workmanlike beauty all its own. Controversial aesthetics apart, the Q.1 was an extremely vigorous freight haulier, as indeed befits what transpired to be the last and most powerful 0-6-0 steam design in this country.

Amongst the inflexible terms of reference handed to Bulleid was the condition that the locomotive should run as fast and as safely in reverse as in forward motion; to this end an effective cab was fitted to the lightly-constructed tender for crew comfort, and in a showmanlike display of the design's running and riding propensities Bulleid himself perched precariously on the coal bunker of a Q.1 whilst speeds upwards of 75m.p.h. were reached in reverse.

The forty Q.1s were assembled in 1942 to a particularly concentrated schedule, and on entering service immediately proved of immense value to the war effort; many remarkable feats of load haulage were achieved over the minor routes for which they had been planned. The total lack of extraneous fittings resulted in unparalleled accessibility for maintenance purposes, and although manufactured at a time of uncertain material quality – and somewhat irregular standards of workmanship – the locomotives were thoroughly reliable and well-liked by their crews.

The strictly inadequate braking system was an early source of anxiety, yet remained untouched since the engines' full power potential generally went unused – at least following ceasefire in 1945. An occasional problem of diminished cab vision by dint of spray thrown up by the unshielded wheels likewise remained unremedied. Very few modifications were adopted throughout the Q.1s' career; externally, the addition of hand-rails to the smokebox front and extra wash-out plugs inset low on the firebox side sheets were the most evident. The innate longevity of the design could have enabled the 0-6-0s, had they been given the opportunity, to work double the number of years they in fact survived. Removal from active service took place between 1963 and 1966, the first Q.1 off the production line being preserved for posterity.

Near the end of its working days, a rust-stained No.33018 reposes outside Eastleigh shed in September 1965. A missing boiler-case plate reveals the feed-water clack valves, and steam injector apparatus is highly visible beneath the cab.
(F. Hornby)

BULLEID Q1 CLASS 0-6-0, 1942

Mechanical lubricator omitted from beneath smokebox

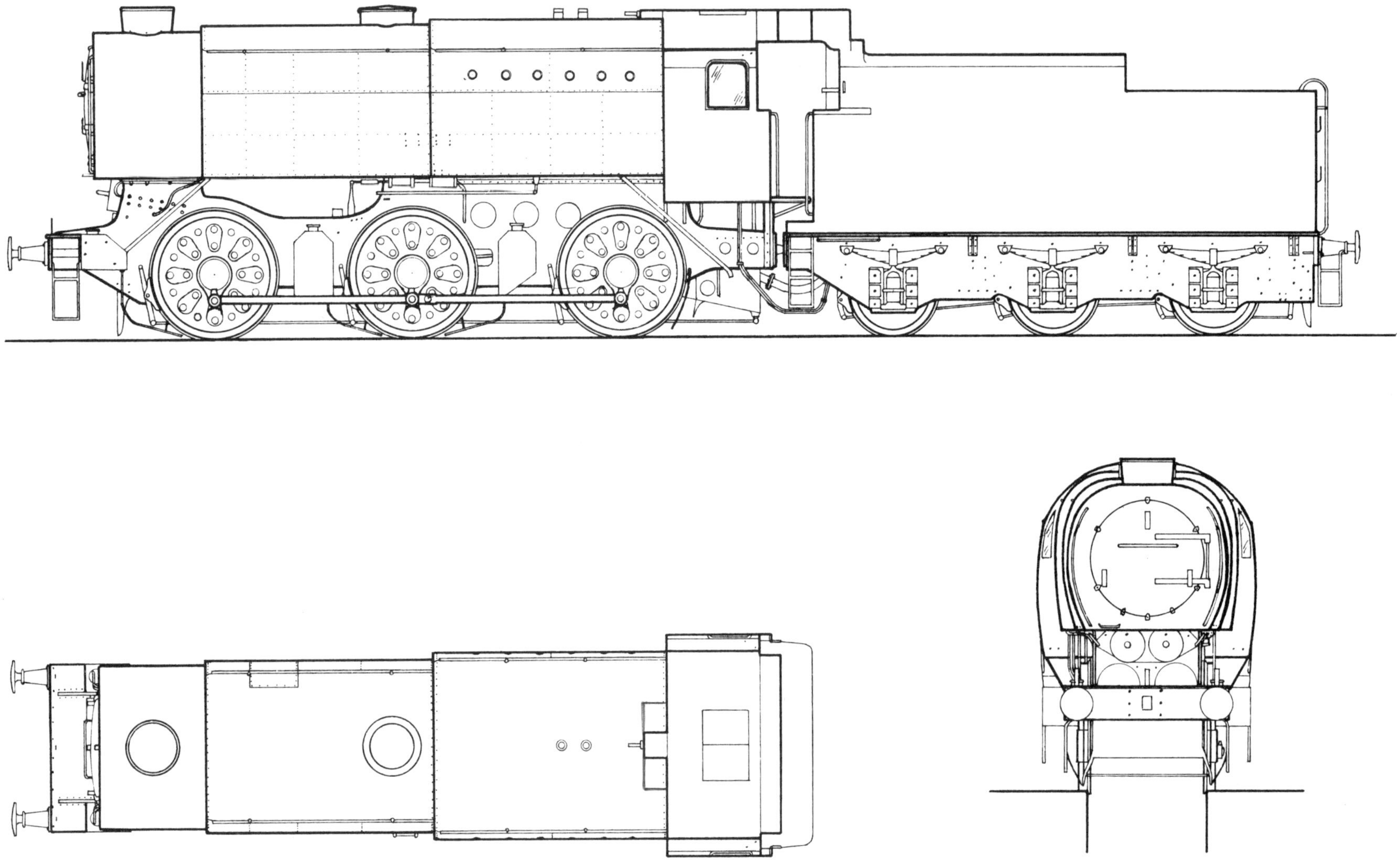

BULLEID Q1 CLASS 0-6-0, 1942

Bulleid had startled a sceptical railway world with the launching of his unprecedented 'Merchant Navy' Class Pacifics, which he had contrived to have had constructed in the austere conditions of 1941 when such grandiose express locomotive schemes, especially those of markedly unusual design, were contrary to wartime requirements. That the 'Merchant Navy' Class was categorised at the design stage as being for mixed traffic usage was an effective sop to the authorities.

The 'West Country' Pacifics were the net result of a need for locomotives of lighter axle loading and thus greater route availability than the 'Merchant Navys', sharing with the latter all major features and the unique 'air-smoothed' boiler cases – Bulleid would not hear of his 4-6-2s described as 'streamlined'. The resultant box-like appearance of the engines earned a variety of nicknames, of which an enduring example was 'Spam Can'.

Assembly took place between 1945 and 1950, in which time 110 locomotives filled the class; seventy were completed by the S.R. and the remainder by B.R. Whilst the majority were christened after localities served by the S.R. in the South West, enormous publicity was gained by adroitly naming 44 lightweight Pacifics after wartime connections with the Battle of Britain. Generally regarded as a separate class, the 'Battle of Britain' locomotives were identical to their confreres in all but nameplates and are therefore collated under the 'West Country' heading for the purposes of this present volume.

Novel features comprised thermic syphons within the firebox to aid rapid steam build-up, successfully employed on European railways but with unremarkable results in Southern application; a welded steel firebox in lieu of the normal copper in view of the very high boiler pressure of 280lbs. per sq. in. (subsequently reset at 250lbs. per sq. in.); a semi-tapered boiler having excellent steaming properties; elaborate Boxpok-type wheels evolved by Bulleid in cooperation with steel manufacturers Firth Brown of Sheffield; 'clasp' brakes operating two brake shoes per wheel; and a unique concept in inside-mounted valve gear incorporating primary drive by chains totally enclosed in an oil bath. The latter was sealed in an attempt to obviate maintenance, an aim that ultimately proved abortive since leakages were a perennial problem.

Bulleid developed this compact motion for his Pacifics since straightforward valve gear could not be accommodated beneath the voluminous boiler, and was further obstructed by the leading coupled axle – the centre axle was driven by all three cylinders, of which the central cylinder was very steeply inclined. The gear functioned admirably when newly installed but progressive chain stretch and allied defects led to inexorable maladjustment and thus unstable valve timing in service. This persistent source of trouble, in addition to a steam reversing gear that proved wildly capricious in usage, under-scored the eventual B.R. decision to rebuild the 4-6-2s.

Primarily intended for passenger work but with an inbuilt ability to handle fitted freight trains if the necessity arose, the lightweight Pacifics were designed to meet the awkward dimensions for working the Hastings line, so that the cabs fitted to the initial batch were several inches slimmer than those of the foregoing 'Merchant Navy' Class. However, since no 4-6-2 ever ventured onto that route, succeeding 'West Countrys' were provided with wider cabs and the earlier versions were later modified accordingly.

54

Much experimenting with boiler casing profiles had taken place on the earliest 'Merchant Navys' and although the finalised shape had basically been arrived at by the time the 'West Countrys' were laid down, the question of effective smoke deflection remained subject to continuing investigation, so that several sizes of deflector plates could be discerned at any one time in the locomotives' lifespan, together with varying styles of cab configuration and front-end panelling.

Battle of Britains were 6" narrower than the West Countries to enable working over the Hastings line. 8'6" and 9' respectively across cabs and tenders

The class as originally outshopped gave magnificent service so long as frequent and efficient maintenance was observed, but they were not easy to drive and required sympathetic handling from drivers; heavy coal consumption and proneness for slipping on take-off went hand in hand with overall performance. Ultimately the mechanical complexity and inflated operating costs of the 'West Countrys' caused B.R. to instigate a systematic and drastic rebuilding programme, to simplify the specification and render improved reliability. Sixty lightweight Pacifics were treated from 1957 until 1961 – when the programme was cancelled owing to withdrawal of steam traction. Between 1963 and 1967 all 110 locomotives were scrapped, with several preservations in both original and rebuilt guises.

In conclusion, these eccentric S.R. 4-6-2s reflected Bulleid's idiosyncratic approach to railway engineering, and by their eye-catching appearance and superb performance when in peak condition helped to revamp the post-war reputation of the S.R.

Backing down to its train with safety valves ajar at Ilfracombe in June 1960 is 'Battle of Britain' Pacific No.34109 'Sir Trafford Leigh Mallory' (the longest name in the class). Note the clean condition, the medium-sized smoke deflectors and A.W.S. battery box atop the buffer beam. *(N.L. Browne)*

BULLEID 'WEST COUNTRY' CLASS 4-6-2, 1945

Leading sander removed soon after construction and cover blocked off.

Modified cab

lance between
r beam and
ders omitted,
ed in early

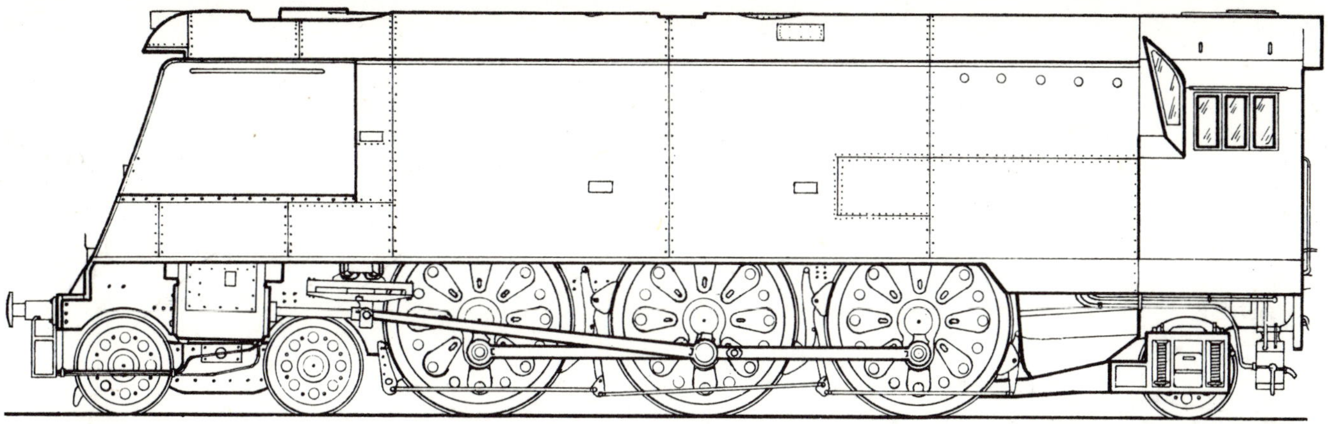

ps and brackets
n in incorrect
ition, protrusion
ront of valves
tted

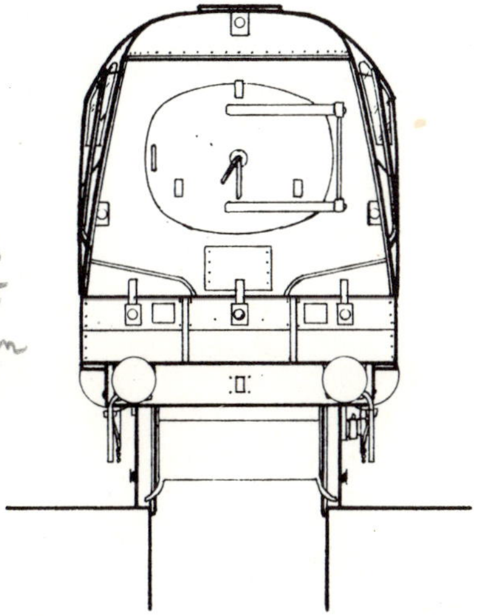

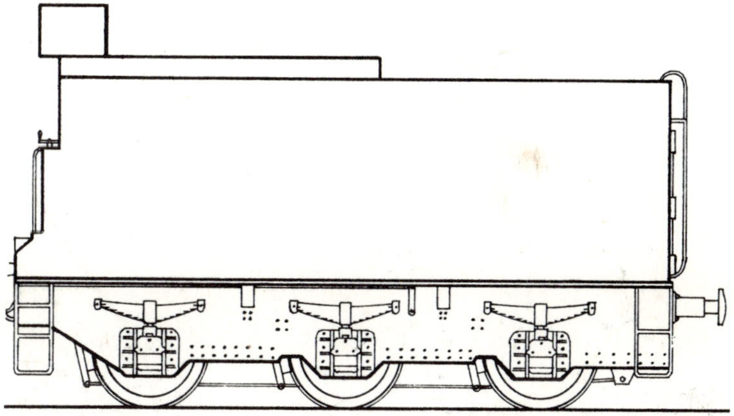

BULLEID 'WEST COUNTRY' CLASS 4-6-2, 1945

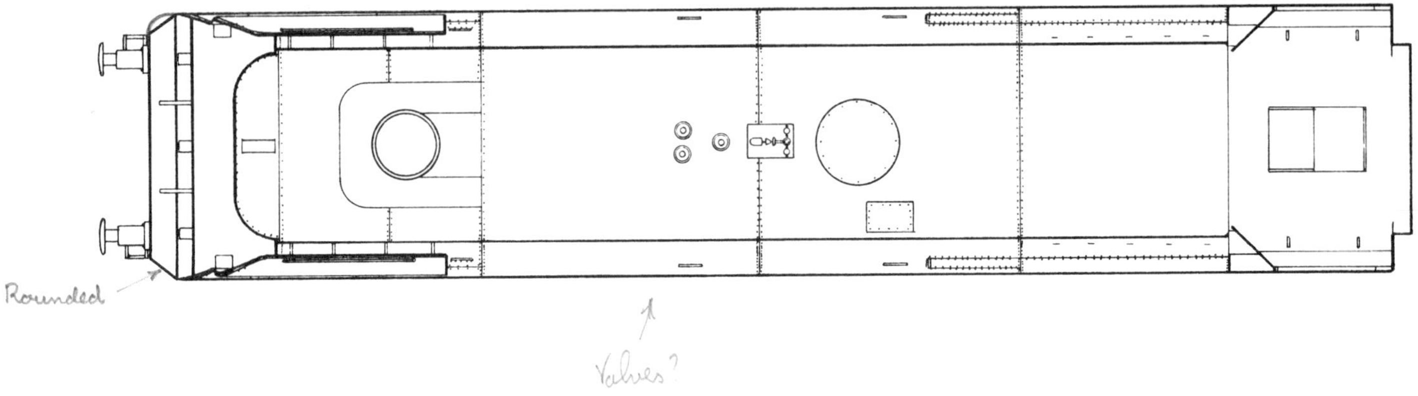

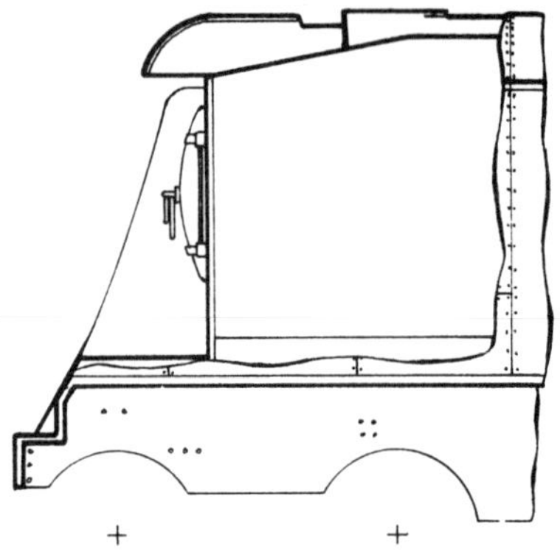

CUT AWAY FRONT CASING,
REVEALING SMOKEBOX SHAPE

56 BULLEID 'WEST COUNTRY' CLASS 4-6-2, 1945

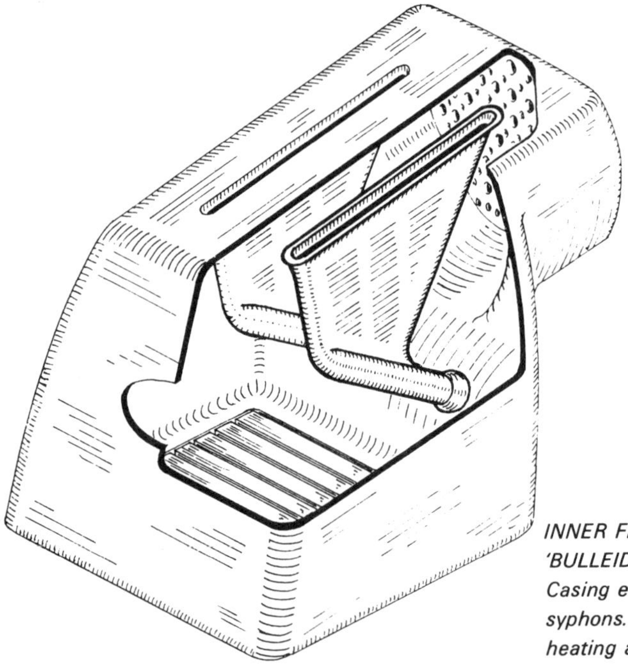

INNER FIREBOX CASING WITH TWIN THERMIC SYPHONS:
'BULLEID PACIFIC'

Casing entirely surrounded by water, which also fills the syphons. Fitted to increase surface area available for heating and to aid water circulation

'West Country' Class nameplate, etc,
Showing nameplate (upper), shield (centre) and class identification plate (lower). View depicts left-hand side fitting: right-hand fitting and location are identical. Length of nameplate varies; shield and class plate standard sizes

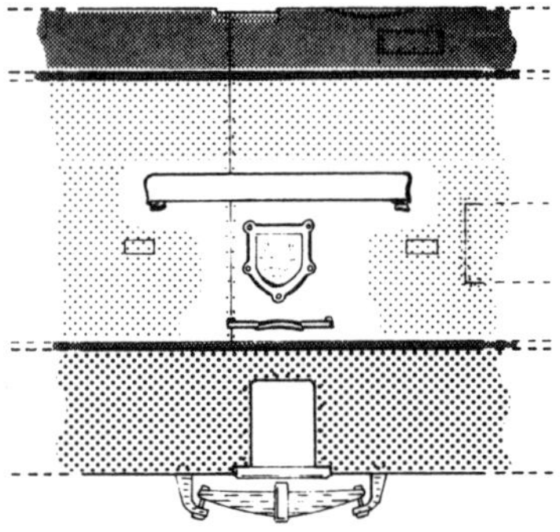

'Battle of Britain' nameplate, etc,
Showing nameplate (upper) and shield. Class identification displayed in base of nameplate. Location comments as above

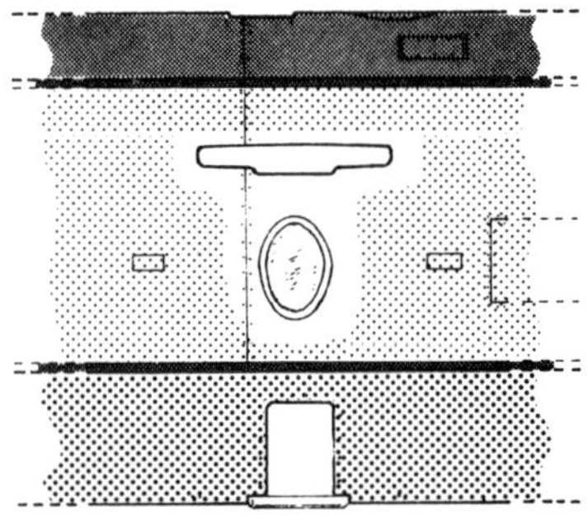

Following the American entry into the European theatre of war during the latter half of World War II, a sizeable number and variety of transatlantic steam locomotives were shipped to England, for transference to the Continent after the D-Day landings. British locomotive engineers and crews were given the opportunity to inspect and operate many of these engines, which, whilst totally alien in character to British designs, vaunted a mass of labour-saving devices such as self-cleaning smokeboxes and rapid-clearing firebox ashpans, that were to prove crucial additions to post-war British locomotives. Specially adapted to clear Continental loading gauges – much less generous than the American equivalents, but giving rise to extremely close encounters with lineside structures when working under the even less tolerant British limits – the engines were designed and built to U.S. Army specifications. Three decades after the general departure of U.S. forces from mainland Europe, the railways of several Balkan countries continued to rely heavily on wartime American steamers, testimony to the high quality of manufacture and inbuilt longevity.

To be expected in such a massive undertaking, the port of Southampton employed a large stud of specially-designed dockyard locomotives, all inherited from the pre-Grouping railways comprising the S.R., of which the vast majority hailed from the L.S.W.R.; by 1945 a considerable proportion of these virile, hard-working but elderly shunters had been exhausted beyond repair by the immense burden of wartime traffic and especially the concentrated build-up to the Normandy invasion in 1944. Rejecting a Bulleid Q.1-based dock-shunting design on the grounds of cost, the S.R. authorities bought on favourable terms fourteen American 0-6-0Ts from the War Department in December 1946.

Designed by the U.S. Army Transportation Corps and built by the American locomotive manufacturers Vulcan and Porter in 1942-43, a consignment of these typical transatlantic shunting engines ('switchers' in U.S. parlance) had been offloaded onto G.W.R. lines in late 1944 and rapidly trans-shipped overseas in the partially dismantled condition in which they arrived. The examples purchased by the S.R. had been placed into W.D. ownership sometime after the war ended in 1945, and before commencing work at Southampton various fitments were modified to meet S.R. specifications.

U.S.A. CLASS 0-6-0T, 1946

Highly unusual to British eyes, these 0-6-0Ts boasted a generous power output that enabled the propulsion of extraordinary loads for their diminutive size. Complete with bar frames, very accessible motion and outside cylinders driving the rear axle, stovepipe chimney, top-feed apparatus (the original single valve of which was later duplicated) and three 'domes' atop the boiler – the first and third were in actuality sand canisters – the aptly-termed 'U.S.A.' Class locomotives were a familiar sight at Southampton for some sixteen years. The commodious cab was a revelation to crews accustomed to distinctly cramped quarters; however, the sheer breadth of the structure was such that diligence was needed on the part of crews when alighting therefrom in the face of oncoming traffic.

Displaced by diesel units in 1963, the survivors beyond that time – withdrawal commenced in 1962 – were dispersed to engine sheds for general purpose duties under the control of district supervisors and thereupon issued with new numbers, until the entire class was finally relieved from any form of service by mid-1967. Curiously, in view of their overt non-British origin – perhaps because of it – no less than four 'U.S.A.' Class 0-6-0Ts have been rescued from obliteration.

In company with others of its genre, a grubby No.DS 233 awaits the call of the scrapyard at Eastleigh in January 1965. Note the large centrally-placed window in the cab front plate and the shunting guide-rod for the driver at the forward edge of the tank. *(F. Hornby)*

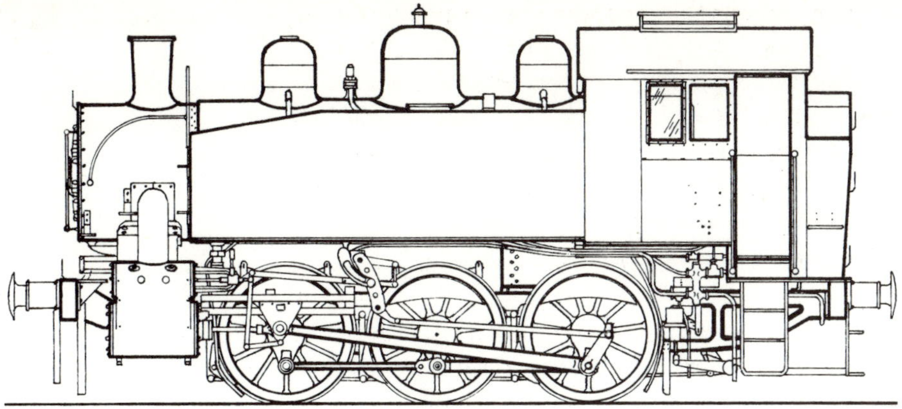

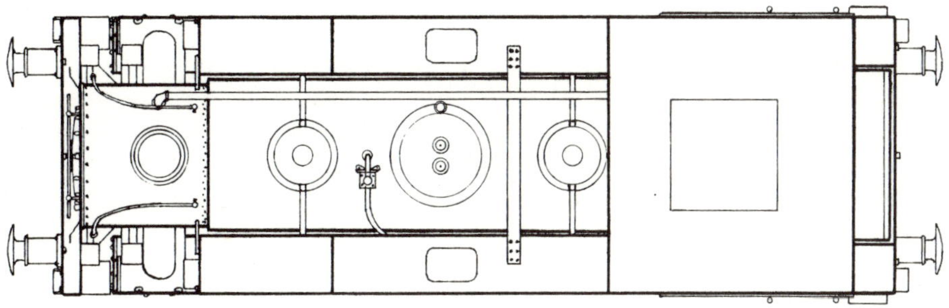

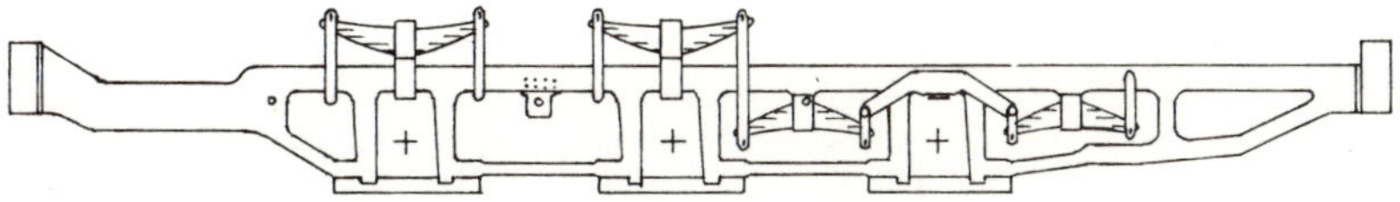

BAR-FRAME STRUCTURE AND SUSPENSION SYSTEM

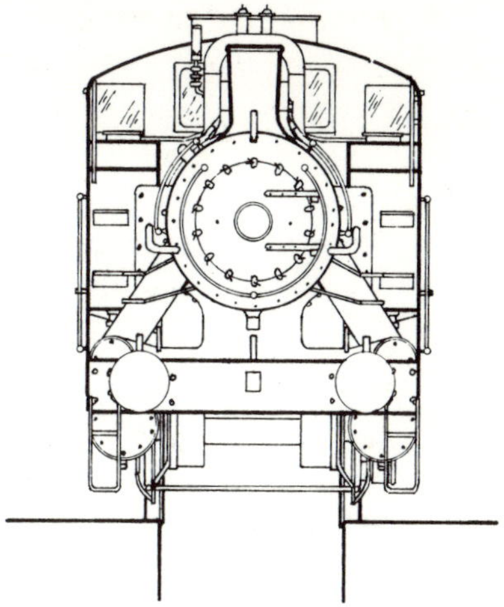

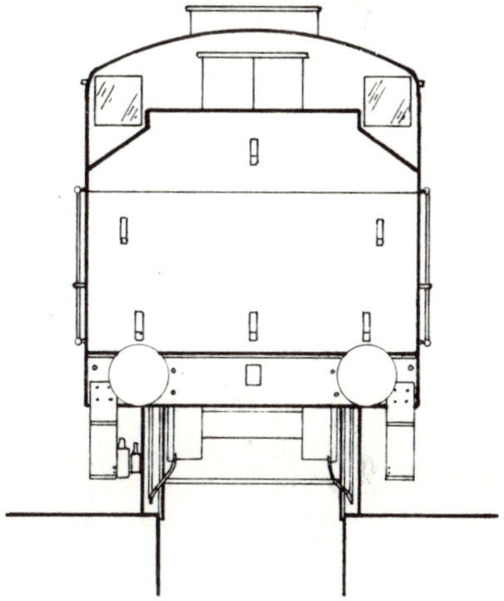

U.S.A. CLASS 0-6-0T, 1946

BULLEID REBUILT 'MERCHANT NAVY' CLASS 4-6-2, 1941-56

Probably the most handsome of latter-day British express steam locomotives, alongside their close cousins the modified 'lightweight' Pacifics, the B.R.-rebuilt 'Merchant Navy' 4-6-2s at first glance do not belong in this survey of S.R. motive power, since some seven years elapsed between dissolution of the Groups and announcement of the rebuilding scheme. However, even though drastically altered internally and externally, a very high percentage of Bulleid-inspired features were retained in the conversion process, thus amply justifying inclusion herein.

From the time of initial outshopping in 1941 until approximately four years later, the revolutionary Bulleid 4-6-2s were so beset with teething problems that at one point their existence was considered an onerous liability. Troubles that were eventually cured included excess weight, exhaust smoke drift, fractured motion shafts, and cracks in the steel fireboxes. The numerous perpetual defects resulting from the ambitious specification – oil bath seepage, chain stretch, temperamental reversing gear and heavy coal consumption, amongst other more minor manifestations – were tolerated in view of the magnificent performances that experienced drivers could wring from them. Thirty 'Merchant Navy' Class Pacifics were constructed, the most troublesome original batch of ten in 1941-42, a second batch of ten improved versions in 1944-45 and the final examples under B.R. auspices in 1948-49; all were named after major shipping lines.

In due course the continuing excessive maintenance demands, aggravated by poor accessibility due to the all-enveloping boiler shells, persuaded the B.R. executive, whose locomotive policy called for mechanical simplification with commensurately reduced levels of maintenance, to institute bold modifications to the hefty Bulleid Pacifics. The sanction for fifteen conversions was issued in 1955 and the first rebuilt 4-6-2 emerged from Eastleigh in February 1956. The successful nature of the modifications was plainly recognisable, so that the order for adapting the remaining fifteen engines was signed in quick succession.

The excellent Bulleid boiler, reduced to 250lbs. per sq. in. maximum pressure and lagged in conventional style, was retained intact, mated to a new smokebox incorporating the original door and crowned by a massive cast-iron chimney (allied to the Lemaître blasting apparatus); the frames, B.F.B. wheels – with additional balance weights – and cab, cut away at the lower sides, were re-used. The most important innovation was the replacement of the problematic Bulleid valve motion by three independent sets of time-proven Walschaerts gear. An accurate screw reversing gear was provided and steam operation of the fire-doors was abandoned.

In 'air-smoothed' guise the Pacifics had been coupled to specially-designed tenders in two basic water tank capacities, 5,000 and 6,000 gallons, of which the latter was the most common. A few years prior to 1956 a programme of tender alteration had been initiated, involving the lowering of side panels and provision of fire-iron tunnels on the larger versions, and the fitting of new 5,250-gallon tanks onto the former 5,000-gallon tender frames. Since this programme terminated during the locomotive rebuilding period, early Pacific conversions were occasionally observed linked to unmodified tenders for a short while.

The effect of the major transformation to the 'Merchant Navy' Class was to render precisely the attributes desired: the locomotives were far simpler to handle and maintain, and were no longer prone to the erratic valve timing phenomena, with imperceptible loss of performance. Mainstays of the longer-distance express service until overrun by diesels, the rebuilt engines inevitably suffered a fundamental change in personality by dint of their less unorthodox guise; nonetheless, the purposeful ebullience of the originals could be conjured up when the occasion arose. The sixty rebuilt light-weight Pacifics evinced similar improvements to their heavier progenitors.

Having gone to the enormous trouble and expense of modifying the 'Merchant Navys' (all thirty were converted over a three-and-a-half year period), B.R. peremptorily scrapped the locomotives between 1964 and 1967 with many years – even decades – of useful life before them. One or two Pacifics existed just five years in remodelled format: a wasteful demise indeed. To be expected of a top link and moreover youthful class, a number of 'Merchant Navys' have escaped the cutting torch, of which No.35028 'Clan Line' (built 1949; rebuilt 1959) undertakes steam specials with panache, whilst No.35029 'Ellerman Lines' survives in sectioned form at the National Railway Museum.

Exuding power even at standstill, the pioneer 1941 Pacific, yet one of the last to be rebuilt (in 1959), No.35001 'Channel Packet' is caught in an impressive pose at Eastleigh sheds in November 1963.
(F. Hornby)

BULLEID REBUILT 'MERCHANT NAVY' CLASS 4-6-2, 1941-56

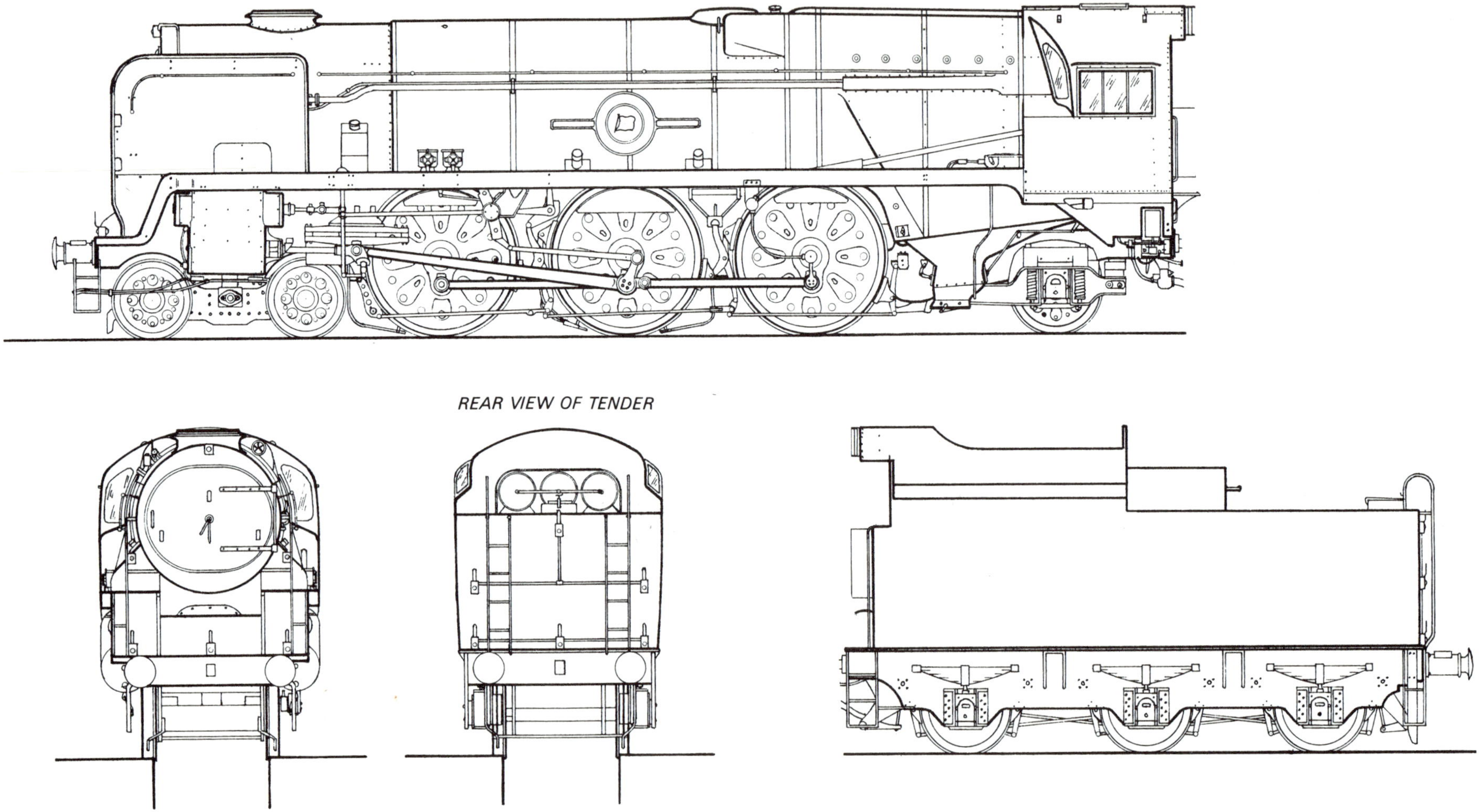

62 BULLEID REBUILT 'MERCHANT NAVY' CLASS 4-6-2, 1941-56

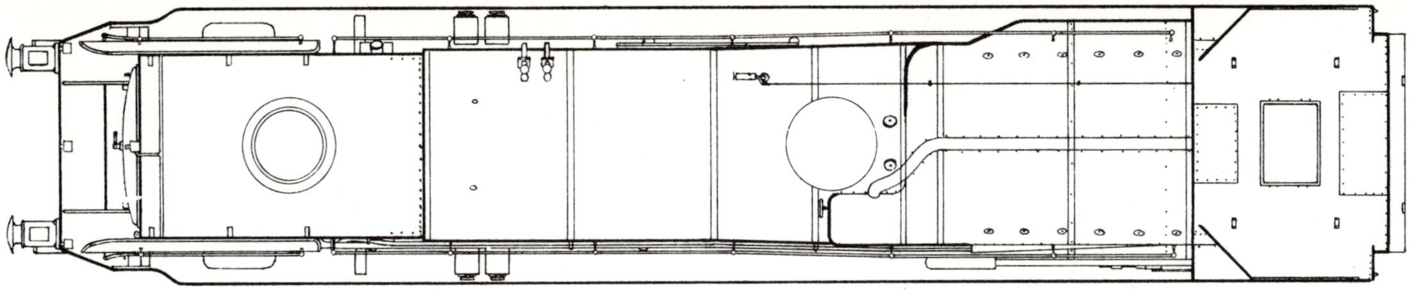

BULLEID REBUILT 'MERCHANT NAVY' CLASS 4-6-2, 1941-56

SECTIONAL VIEW SHOWING FRAME LAYOUT, DISPOSITION OF SMOKEBOX AND FIREBOX RELATIVE TO FRAME AND FOOTPLATE RESPECTIVELY. FRAME DETAILS IDENTICAL TO ORIGINAL VERSION AND SIMILAR TO LIGHT-WEIGHT PACIFICS

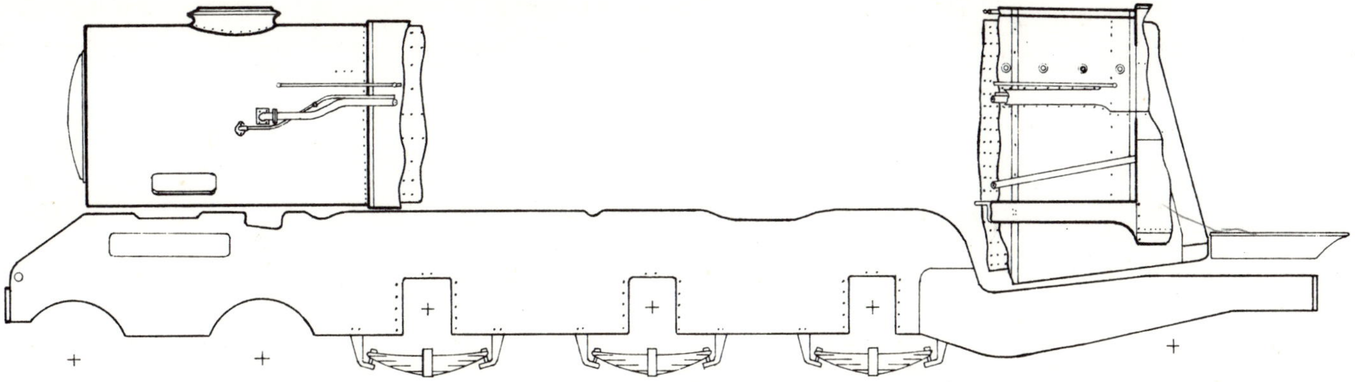